The Millionaire Christian

The Millionaire Christian

PROFITING
FROM SPIRITUAL
CAPITAL DURING
CHALLENGING TIMES

FELICIA M. GILLIE-JACKSON

©2011 by Felicia M. Gillie-Jackson
2nd Printing 2014.

Trusted Books is an imprint of Deep River Books. The views expressed or implied in this work are those of the author. To learn more about Deep River Books, go online to www.DeepRiverBooks.com.

No part of this publication may be reproduced, stored in a retrieval system or transmitted in any way by any means—electronic, mechanical, photocopy, recording or otherwise—without the prior permission of the Publisher, except as provided by USA copyright law.

The author of this book has waived the publisher's suggested editing. As such, the author is responsible for any errors found in this finished product.

Unless otherwise noted, all Scriptures are taken from the *King James Version* of the Bible.

ISBN: 978-1-63269-397-6
Library of Congress Catalog Card Number: 2011921818

To my husband, Lance C. Jackson Sr., you are my best friend. I praise God for blessing me with His best. To my children, Melanie, Victoria, and Christie, thank you for accepting the sacrifice of time it took for God to work His project through me. To my parents, Fegan and Louvenia Gillie, my devoted thanks for your encouragement and for exemplifying faith during challenging times.

Contents

Acknowledgments ix

Foreword xi

Introduction xv
  Profiting From Spiritual Capital During Challenging Times
  Spiritual Capital—The Christian Alternative
  About This Book

Key Attribute 1: Prayer-Praise-Power Is Spiritual Capital . . 1
  Prayer Reveals The Source
  Prayer Reveals Expectancy
  Praise Reveals Agreement With God
  Praise Reveals No Compromises
  Praise Reveals "The Victim Role"
  Power Reveals All Possibilities
  Power Reveals Renewable Energy
  Review Questions

Key Attribute 2 : Commitment Is Spiritual Capital...... 27
Review Questions

Key Attribute 3: Contentment Is Spiritual Capital 35
Review Questions

Key Attribute 4 : Confidence Is Spiritual Capital 43
Review Questions

Key Attribute 5: Self-Forgiveness Is Spiritual Capital 51
Review Questions

Key Attribute 6: Vision Is Spiritual Capital............ 63
Review Questions

Key Attribute 7: Faith Is Spiritual Capital............. 71
Review Questions

Key Attribute 8: Knowledge Is Spiritual Capital 79
The Conversion Life Experience
The Cleansing Life Experience
The Conviction Life Experience
The Correction Life Experience
Review Questions

Key Attribute 9: Wisdom Is Spiritual Capital 105
Review Questions

Key Attribute 10: Sovereignty Is Spiritual Capital...... 115
Review Questions

Summary................................... 125
Printable Supervision Journal
Printable 90 Day Prayer Journal
Printable Recommitment Journal
Affirmations

Acknowledgments

THANKFUL RECOGNITION TO: Dr. Joyce Gillie-Cruse, Louvenia Gillie-Timms, Denise L. Carter, Tracy Gathers, Tiffany Mack, Val Pierce, and Carrie Mack. To my brother, Fegan Gillie Jr., I love you.

Special thanks to Jacqueline Gillie-Buntyn, Pastor Marlon Young, Debra A. Gillie, Linda J. Gillie-Batchelor, and Willard and Elnora Jackson for contributing to Kingdom Building.

With sincere love and deep appreciation

—Felicia M. Gillie-Jackson

Foreword

IN HEBREWS 11, in a dialogue believers affectionately refer to as "the faith chapter," the writer shares these words:

> *"Now faith is the substance of things hoped for,*
> *the evidence of things not seen.*
> *For by it the elders obtained a good report."*

As though perched high in the press box of some huge coliseum, the author pronounces a litany of extraordinary exploits accomplished by ordinary men and women *"by faith."* Then suddenly, in the midst of the resounding roll call—between Enoch's translation and Noah's building of the Ark—the writer pauses, and invokes the following disclaimer:

> *"But without faith [it is] impossible to please [him]: for he that cometh to God must believe that he is, and [that] he is a rewarder of them that diligently seek him."*
>
> —Hebrews 11:6

With this simple statement, this author reveals a nonetheless significant truth: that pleasing God is a two-fold process. First, there is the matter of believing that God exists, and second, there is the matter of believing that God is faithful, that He will come through! In other words, having faith in God requires more than just believing, it requires that the believer possess sufficient determination to endure, to see his or her way through life's difficulties until they arrive at the blessings that await them once those difficulties have passed. Put another way, it is impossible to please God without a faith that is assured that come what may, the Lord *will* make a way somehow!

Still, just how *does* a person trust God when they are in trouble? How does one maintain their *trust* in God when they cannot *trace* Him, when they cannot read the sentence His mighty hand has written? The story of Job provides a timeless and worthwhile answer.

Although Job was a man of great means, we do not remember him because of his wealth. We remember him for his abundance of faith—his resolve to maintain his trust in God when everything else that he treasured was gone. The reason we revere Job's faith is not so much that he continued to believe in God's existence, but rather that through his words and actions, Job himself remained faithful to God until God, in the end, came through!

There is invaluable currency in maintaining such a faith in God that no matter how disillusioning one's circumstance, one's resolve to please God, nevertheless, remains undiminished. Once the believer deposits such riches in his or her heart, they possess a priceless treasure, an eternally durable dividend that yields the capacity to persevere through every vicissitude of life. Such treasure defines the essence of *The Millionaire Christian*.

Foreword

Currency as a metaphor for Christian commitment is nothing new to the nomenclature of faith. In Luke 14:28, for example, Jesus inquires, *"For which of you, intending to build a tower, sitteth not down first, and counteth the cost, whether he have [sufficient] to finish [it]?"* In another place, Matthew 5:3, Jesus begins the Beatitudes with the words, *"Blessed are the poor in spirit, for theirs is the kingdom of heaven".* While the valuation of which Jesus speaks here is not a measure of money but a measure of humility (the *"poor in spirit"* being those who are humble enough to know that they need God), the question of wealth, whether metaphoric or literal, is common in Scripture.

For instance, in another place, Luke 6:24, Jesus speaks quite literally: *"Woe unto you that are rich! For ye have received your consolation."* Although his words might be lost on a world deafened by the incessant drumbeat of modern-day prosperity doctrine, Jesus speaks with clarity and authority, unmistakably distinguishing kingdom principles from worldly ones and issuing a strong warning against seeking wealth as an end unto itself. The Apostle Paul adds further clarity on this point: *"Charge them that are rich in this world, that they be not highminded, nor trust in uncertain riches, but in the living God, who giveth us richly all things to enjoy"* (1 Timothy 6:17).

This is not to suggest that it is either virtuous or holy to be poor. Rather, it is to say that there is a greater wealth than the wealth of this world and that person whose faith is true recognizes the proper relative values and virtues of the two. Whether Job or the modern-day believer, the man or woman of faith places far greater value on the things of God than they place on the things of this world. They *"lay up for [themselves] treasures in heaven, where neither moth nor rust doth corrupt, and where thieves do not break through nor steal"* (Matthew 6:20).

In this book, *The Millionaire Christian*, Felicia Jackson uniquely captures the fact that the richer person is not necessarily the one who has acquired greater financial wealth. Rather, it is that individual who, despite their financial condition, is, as James 2:5 states, *"rich in faith,"* and lives in the certainty that they are *"heirs of the kingdom [God] has promised to them."*

This is the personal and sometimes poignant work of a true Millionaire Christian. Drawing upon her own experiences as well as scriptural examples, Mrs. Jackson brings much-needed refreshment, encouragement, and hope to the millions of other Millionaire Christians out there who have discovered *"we have this treasure in earthen vessels"*. This book is for all of the ordinary men and women of God, believers who are accomplishing extraordinary things by faith day by day and thereby adding their names to that pantheon we know as the *"great cloud of witnesses."*

—**André O. Williams**
Whole City Ministries USA

Introduction

Profiting From Spiritual Capital During Challenging Times

AT THE TIME of this writing, the world is facing economic turmoil. The unemployment rate is skyrocketing and crime is steadily on the rise. Murders and robberies have escalated so high that local city officials are in constant dialogue with police chiefs pondering ways to reduce crime on the streets. The police themselves are baffled and somewhat stunned at the fact that someone could shoot and kill a fellow police officer, in uniform, for some kind of monetary gain. Family suicide has surfaced as a new trend. Husbands are killing their wives and parents are killing their children. There's not enough money to pay the bills and take care of the family at the same time. Therefore, the decision is made to eliminate the burden—so the entire family dies.

The bottom line: it's all about money. The truth of the matter is that when you have no money and no access to money, life takes on a different meaning. Think about it. Imagine yourself in your current lifestyle (spouse, children, house, and everything you currently have), and suddenly you have no money and no access to money. Is the thought unbearable? Life is good when you have money and have access to money. But honestly, what would you do if you were, as some would say, "broke"—not a penny in your pocket? Would you kill for money? I don't believe anyone said when they were a child, "When I grow up, I want to kill my entire family." What is it about money that would make some people think the unthinkable and do the unbelievable? You don't think that money could ever control you? Never say never.

When it comes to money, the ultimate quest in the world today is the quest for capital. Capital is an investment terminology. A baseline definition is "money generates money." A more familiar definition is "it takes money to make money." The Internet and television are flooded with so many "get rich quick" tactics that even Christians are taking what little money they have and resorting to formulas and scams to get what they call "unclaimed capital." I hear so often, "It's time to name it and claim it—the devil had it long enough". I guess that type of thinking would be acceptable if you believe that money is the answer to challenging times. However, if you believe that God is the answer to challenging times, then your quest is not for financial capital but for Spiritual Capital.

For the purpose of this book, Spiritual Capital is a key attribute that enables Christians to live a life of victory during challenging times. Challenging times can be devastating. If there's no counter reaction or wall of defense, challenging times will deteriorate the spiritual, mental, physical, and emotional being. For Christians, Spiritual Capital is that counter reaction and

Introduction

wall of defense. The problem is that many Christians don't profit from Spiritual Capital during challenging times. Therefore, they become overwhelmed and confused. The end result is spiritual death—a separation from God by way of ignoring God or spiritually disconnecting from every believer, including family and friends. It is imperative to survival for Christians to profit from Spiritual Capital during challenging times.

Spiritual Capital—The Christian Alternative

Growing up as a child, I remember dreaming about living the life of a millionaire. I remember telling my mother that I was going to buy her a fur coat and a brand new Cadillac for my father. Have you ever thought about living the life of a millionaire? What would you buy? Ask yourself, "*Is money important to me?*"

Children are taught the "power" of money. At an early age, a child learns that money is the tool used to get the things they want and the things that they need. Children witness the happiness money produces when accessible, and the frustrations when the checkbook is at zero balance. Adults equate money with happiness and believe the more money they have, the happier they will be. What started out as a consideration for trade purposes has now evolved to be a vital and life-sustaining necessity. For some, money has become a refuge, a very present help in the time of trouble. Wait a minute—isn't that supposed to be God?

People have ascribed power to money that money should not have. Through people, money has the power to make friends, destroy families, and change emotions. Money is so powerful that merely thinking about having more of it produces temporary joy and fulfillment with life. Years ago, life's satisfaction consisted of keeping a couple of dollars in your pocket. Today, people aren't satisfied until they become millionaires. The life of a millionaire is viewed as a powerful and glamorous life. To an outsider looking in, a millionaire experiences no troubles, no worries, and definitely no challenges. They have financial capital, which is the answer to all of their problems. Financial capital is to millionaires as Spiritual Capital is to Christians. Whereas financial capital positions millionaires to rely on money as their answer, Spiritual Capital positions Christians to rely on God as their answer. So, if you are a Christian, consider yourself a millionaire—a Millionaire Christian!

During challenging times, Spiritual Capital is the Christian's alternative. Three examples of Spiritual Capital found in the Bible are: (1) Jesus in the garden of Gethsemane, (2) the woman with an issue of blood, and (3) David fleeing from his son Absalom. When in the garden called Gethsemane, Jesus faced a challenging time. As His crucifixion drew near, "being in an agony he prayed more earnestly: and his sweat was as it were great drops of blood falling down to the ground" (Luke 22:44). With thoughts of the cross before Him, Jesus' soul was overwhelmed with sorrow. Nonetheless He was *committed* to the Father and prayed, "Thy will be done" (Matthew 26:42). During challenging times, *commitment* is Spiritual Capital.

The woman with a twelve-year issue of blood faced a challenging time. She sought many doctors for healing, and after spending all of her money she was not healed but yet grew worse. When she heard of Jesus, she pressed through the crowd, "For she said, If I may touch but his clothes, I shall be whole"

Introduction

(Mark 5:28). After touching Jesus' garment, "straightway the fountain of her blood was dried up; and she felt in her body that she was healed of that plague" (Mark 5:29). Jesus, recognizing that power had left Him, turned to the woman, "and he said unto her, Daughter, thy *faith* hath made thee whole; go in peace, and be whole of thy plague" (v. 34). During challenging times, *faith* is Spiritual Capital.

David faced a challenging time. After a long confrontation with Saul, David finally took his seat as king of Israel. In the course of time, David's son Absalom conspired to steal the throne from his father.

> "And Absalom rose up early, and stood beside the way of the gate: and it was so, that when any man had a controversy came to the king for judgment, then Absalom called unto him, and said, Of what city art thou? And he said, Thy servant is of one of the tribes of Israel. And Absalom said unto him, See, thy matters are good and right; but there is no man *deputed* of the king to hear thee. Absalom said morever, Oh that I were made judge in the land, that every man which hath any suit or cause might come unto me, and I would do him justice!"
> —2 Samuel 15:2-4

With these smooth and subtle words, Absalom won the hearts of Israel, and David had to flee in order to save his life. While running for his life and running from his son, David turned to God and said: "But thou, O Lord, art a shield for me; my glory, and the lifter of mine head" (Psalm 3:3). During a challenging time, David *praised* God. *Praise* is Spiritual Capital.

About This Book

If you purchased this book because you thought this was a "get rich quick" book, you were so wrong. Sadly, many Christians believe that if they had millions of dollars they could withstand the negative pressures of life and be a better husband or a better wife, a better person, and a stronger Christian. Not true. What is true? Profiting from Spiritual Capital is what makes a better husband, a better wife, a better person, and a stronger Christian.

Challenges come in many forms, whether sickness, strife, or threat of poverty. We profit from Spiritual Capital when we respond to these challenges in a manner consistent with the way that Jesus would respond and in a manner that Jesus would approve of. Where the world chooses money as a defense, Christians choose Spiritual Capital.

Spiritual Capital:

- ❖ Preserves the Christian's soul during challenging times
- ❖ Predicts the Christian's responses and reactions to challenging times
- ❖ Is scripturally-based
- ❖ Illuminates God's end result to every challenging moment. God's end result is victory.

This book contains ten Key Spiritual Attributes that guarantee the Christian's right to prosperity and victory. When we select these Spiritual Attributes as our defense, they convert to Spiritual Capital and yield recovery and restoration. Each Attribute is biblically-based. In addition, each Attribute engages

Introduction

the reader by using examples of challenges experienced by people in the Bible and referencing several of the author's personal challenges. Inside this book, you will find:

- A set of review questions to help you with personalizing and internalizing each Key Attribute.
- Affirmation Statements designed to:

  ➢ Increase your focus on the scriptures
  ➢ Promote your spiritual growth
  ➢ Increase your faith

- A 90 Day Prayer Journal to allow you, the reader, to convert general prayers to specific prayer requests. In addition, the journal includes a daily commentary for you to keep track of God's answers.
- An End of the Day Meditation and Review Journal designed to help you to:

  ➢ Establish God's order for your day
  ➢ Set God's vision for your day
  ➢ Set goals for your ministry

- A Daily Recommitment Journal to help you reaffirm and rekindle your love for Jesus Christ.

This book is your personal diary. Write in this book, cry in this book, and heal in this book. No matter what challenge you are facing, be it financial, marital, professional, or family, you are a Millionaire Christian and it is time to take your position. Are you ready? If so, then

 **PROCEED TO THE NEXT PAGE**

KEY ATTRIBUTE 1

Prayer-Praise-Power Is Spiritual Capital

THE FIRST KEY Attribute is a combination of three Attributes: Prayer, Praise, and Power. They are so important yet so intertwined that they are combined into one Key Attribute. However, they will be discussed separately and in the following order:

Prayer

- o   Reveals The Source
- o   Reveals Expectancy

Praise

- o   Reveals Agreement With God
- o   Reveals No Compromises
- o   Reveals The "Victim Role"

Power

- o   Reveals All Possibilities
- o   Reveals Renewable Energy

"Pray without ceasing."
—I Thessalonians 5:17

Prayer

Prayer Reveals The Source

We are instructed to pray without ceasing. The word "pray" in I Thessalonians 5:17 is *proseuchomai* in the Greek, and it means to entreat—to urgently and earnestly petition God. This type of prayer is personal and specific. It reflects total dependence on God. "Without ceasing" means prayer is our Christian duty. Prayer is required. Therefore, we never neglect to pray. We are obligated to pray.

We pray without ceasing because prayer reveals God as our Source. I remember when I worked for a non-profit organization. After six years of employment, God planted in my spirit that it was time to move on. I said okay, and waited for further instructions. Actually, I was waiting for the new job to appear. I was always told that God doesn't close one door

> *Prayer is a spirit detoxifier—spirit cleanser. Prayer brings to the surface everything that stands in opposition to the will of God for our lives.*

without opening another one. How not true. Nonetheless, I waited for an open door before I resigned.

The message to resign was pounding in my spirit. I said, "Okay, God, I hear you. Where's the open door? What job will I transfer to?" I said to God, "You sound like you want me to quit this job without having another one." He said, "Yes." I told God, "I can't quit this job. This job is my bread and butter—my Source." God replied, "I thought I was your bread and butter—your Source." Man, I felt bad. Repentance was not enough to settle the pain I felt and the disappointment I received from God. I cried and I wanted to run away—run away from His presence.

Sometimes life can make us feel as though we are in control. Our drive to survive evolves around meeting our daily needs and wants. Our pursuit is to make life easy and our goal is to live in the "comfort zone." The comfort zone is dangerous living. The comfort zone hinders us from walking by faith. We live in the comfort zone when job, family, and leisure time function harmoniously together. It is when we have life down to a routine with no disappointments or surprises. In the comfort zone, God is only included to give that "perfect Christian" picture. Moreover, God has a place—it's called "church," and we make every attempt to visit Him on Sundays when fulfilling our religious duty. Quality time with God consists of consulting Him on an "as needed" basis. The comfort zone feeds the assumption that we are in control and we make things happen. We dictate how life is supposed to be. We make the choices and we assume credit for the outcomes. In essence, we are the source.

During challenging times, it's difficult for us to leave our comfort zone. Although we feel secure, it is a false security, but nonetheless we feel protected. Living in the comfort zone teaches us to minimize stress by blocking out reality. We stick to our selfish motives by constantly rehearsing in our minds the refusal to allow anyone *to steal our joy*.

The Millionaire Christian lives contrary to the comfort zone. The Millionaire Christian has identified the "comfort zone" as a trick from the enemy and refuses to become stagnated. The Millionaire Christian lives a life of prayer. Prayer is a spirit detoxifier—spirit cleanser. Prayer brings to the surface everything that stands in opposition to the will of God for our lives. Prayer removes us from the comfort zone and restores the function of the Holy Spirit—to lead us and to guide us. Prayer cultivates total dependency on God. Praying without ceasing reveals that God is the Source. When God is our Source, our lives function from the premise that everything originates from and culminates with God. He is the Sole Provider.

> *"Be careful for nothing; but in every thing by prayer and supplication with thanksgiving let your requests be made know unto God. And the peace of God, which passeth all understanding, shall keep your hearts and minds through Christ Jesus."*
> —Philippians 4:6-7

Prayer Reveals Expectancy

Prayer has purpose. One purpose of prayer (which I have heard time and time again) is to communicate with and to God. Although that purpose may work for some, I have come to learn that prayer encompasses more than merely communicating with and to God. For example, I have Caller ID on my telephone.

Therefore, while my telephone is ringing, I can see all the incoming telephone numbers before answering. People would often say to me, "Felicia I called you today," I would respond by saying, "I saw your number on my Caller ID but I did not hear a message." They would respond, "Oh, I didn't leave a message." I would quickly respond with, "Then you didn't call me. You just dialed my number." What would prompt someone to pick up the telephone and dial someone's telephone number? In short, expectancy!

When we attempt to make a telephone call, we either expect that person to answer, to not answer, or we expect to hear their voicemail message. Nonetheless, we had a need, we dialed their telephone number, and we expected a response. Therefore, to attempt a telephone call with no expectations whatsoever is just dialing their telephone number. The same with prayer; prayer involves more than communicating with and to God. Prayer contains expectation. To voice words to God and not expect anything from Him (in my opinion) is not prayer, it is talking. Moreover, God did not say that He would answer our elaborate talking. God said that He would answer our prayers. Prayer doesn't end after the "amen." That's just the beginning. Prayer continues through expectancy.

The Millionaire Christian lives a life of expectancy through prayer. The Millionaire Christian prays and EXPECTS God to answer.

Prayer works like a boomerang, a curved stick that when thrown returns to the thrower. The person throwing the boomerang expects the boomerang to return. Why? Well, because that's the boomerang's design. That's the boomerang's purpose. As it is when throwing a boomerang, when prayer is released, the person praying expects something in return—expects something to happen. That's the design of prayer. That's the purpose of prayer. Psalm 62:5 reads: "My soul, wait thou only upon God; for my expectation is from him." When we pray without ceasing, we always stay in a state of expectancy. Our expectation is from God at all times and at any given time. The Millionaire Christian lives a life of expectancy through prayer. The Millionaire Christian prays and EXPECTS God to answer.

The Millionaire Christian profits from Spiritual Capital.
During challenging times,
Prayer
Acknowledging God as the Source with GREAT expectations
Is
Spiritual Capital

"Seven times a day do I praise thee because of thy righteous judgments."
—Psalm 119:164

Praise

Praise Reveals Agreement With God

Psalm 22 is notably referred to as the Psalm of the Cross. It has been stated that this Psalm may have been recited by Jesus while on the cross. If so, this Psalm gives a clear and vivid picture into the mind of Christ. His thoughts echo throughout the 31 verses. The question is asked, "Why, God, have you forsaken me?" In other words, *It wasn't supposed to be like this. I thought I was supposed to be the head and not the tail. I thought I was supposed to be above and never beneath. This is not how we planned it.* Have you ever been there? Have you found yourself at a point in time that was not supposed to be? The pain—the tears—you want to cry out, "God, where are you? Are you angry with me? Are you punishing me? Won't you tell me my faults? Where did I go wrong? My God, my God, why have you forsaken me?"

During challenging times, God seems a million miles away. We pray and pray and it appears as though God does not hear our prayers. The truth of the matter is God's answer to our prayers was not the answer we were looking for. Therefore, instead of focusing on God, we focus on the answer and become discouraged. We feel as though our trials will never end. To compound matters, the enemy tries to convince us to believe we are living cursed instead of living blessed. Feeling forsaken, we position God as the cause of our turmoil and distress. We question Him and we demand Him to explain: "What's going on? Why is this happening to me?"

If Rebekah were here to testify, she would say, "Amen." Remember the story of Rebekah and how she wanted to have children? Rebekah's story is found in Genesis 25. The chapter talks about the birth of Jacob and Esau. Verse 21 reads, "And Isaac entreated the Lord for his wife, because she was barren: and the Lord was entreated of him, and Rebekah his wife conceived." The Bible continues to say that the pregnancy did not go as expected as the two children struggled in her womb. Rebekah asked God, "If it be so, why am I thus?" (v. 22). Rebekah was otherwise saying, "If you have answered my prayer, then why is my situation going so wrong? Why is my life like this?" The struggle within her womb was not what Rebekah expected. Paraphrasing, Rebekah was saying, "God, I did everything you told me to do. I'm not a bad person. You said to make my request known unto You and I did. Where are you? God, if you have answered my prayer, then why is my life like this? Why is my life like this?"

> *Praise keeps us in a state of spiritual agreement with God.*

Rebekah was in it for Rebekah. She wanted children and she prayed for children. In Rebekah's opinion, the pregnancy brought forth grief. However, God responded to Rebekah by saying that two nations were within her womb, and the separation of two peoples had begun in her body. God answered her prayer according to His will. Where Rebekah saw children, God saw two nations.

Praise keeps us in a state of spiritual agreement with God. Spiritual agreement with God was the goal of the writer of Psalm 22. The writer was feeling forsaken. It is evident that things were not going as planned. Yet verses 22-23 read: "I will declare thy name unto my brethren: in the midst of the congregation will I praise thee. Ye that fear the Lord, praise him; all ye the seed of Jacob glorify him; and fear him, all ye the seed of Israel." The writer concluded that even when life seems as though it is going contrary to the will of God and nothing seems to be going right, his spirit will agree with God.

Prayer-Praise-Power Is Spiritual Capital

Praise is our spiritual gauge used to monitor, measure, and maintain spiritual agreement with God. When we are in spiritual agreement with God, doors that appear closed are actually opened, and answers to prayers that appear to contradict our request are precisely what we asked for. When life is not going as expected and answered prayers take us from joy to grief, praise keeps us on that narrow road that leads to life. We exist in harmony with God and we behold His presence.

> *"Therefore I love thy commandments above gold; yea, above fine gold."*
> —Psalm 119:127

Praise Reveals No Compromises

Praise leaves no room to compromise the will of God. Praise intensifies the power and presence of God—which in turn overrule any and all selfish motives and intents. We humbly surrender to God and seek nothing but His desires and His plans for our lives. Nehemiah is an example of somebody who refused to compromise the will of God. Writing during a time when Israel's rebellion separated them from God and landed them in captivity, Nehemiah's name means "Jehovah comforts." After many years in captivity, a remnant of the captives was granted permission to return to Jerusalem. For some time after their return, although the temple was rebuilt, the wall had not been rebuilt, nor were the gates restored. When Nehemiah learned of this, he was saddened and burdened in his heart. God graced Nehemiah to return to Jerusalem to oversee the rebuilding project.

During the rebuilding effort, some enemies (specifically Sanballat, Tobiah, and Geshem) were angry and caused trouble for Nehemiah. They were jealous and wanted the work to stop. However, Nehemiah was a man that followed after the will of God and did not let the sparks from the enemy intimidate him. Sanballat and Geshem sent a message asking Nehemiah to meet together in one of the villages on the plain of Ono. Nehemiah responded that he was doing a "great" work and could not come down. Sanballat and Geshem sent their message four times, and four times Nehemiah responded the same. If this was not enough, Sanballat started a rumor and tried to blackmail Nehemiah to stop the work. However, Nehemiah prayed and asked God to strengthen his hands so the work would not stop. Nonetheless, the enemy would stop at nothing until the work was halted. So Shemaiah, the son of Delaiah, the son of Mehetabeel, said to Nehemiah, "Let us meet together in the house of God, within the temple, and let us shut the doors of the temple: for they will come to slay thee; yea, in the night will they come to slay thee" (Nehemiah 6:10). Nehemiah responded that he would not go in as he perceived that Shemaiah had not been sent by God but was hired by Tobiah and Sanballat.

> *The Millionaire Christian refuses to compromise the will of God. The Millionaire Christian doesn't back out or back away from the will of God for fear or threats from their enemies. God's plan is the final and only plan.*

God's will was for the wall to be rebuilt and the gates restored. Nehemiah refused to compromise the will of God. It was God's way or no way. When confronted by the enemy, Nehemiah measured their word against the will of God. When the enemy said, "Come let's meet," Nehemiah said, "I must rebuild the wall and restore the gates." When the enemy used blackmail and lies, Nehemiah said, "I must rebuild the wall and restore the gates." When the enemy said, "Hide and save your life," Nehemiah said, "I must rebuild the wall and restore the gates." Each and every time Nehemiah was presented with an opportunity to forsake the will of God, he surrendered to the will of God.

Nehemiah's refusal to compromise God's will resulted in praise during a challenging time. Heads that were hung low were uplifted and dying spirits were restored to life. The presence of God was rekindled and the Israelites praised God so heavily that the celebration outranked all celebrations since the days of Joshua. There was GREAT gladness! (Nehemiah 8:16-17).

The Millionaire Christian refuses to compromise the will of God. The Millionaire Christian doesn't back out or back away from the will of God for fear or threats from their enemies. God's plan is the final and only plan. During challenging times, the Millionaire Christian resorts to praise and stays in the presence of God while He perfects His plan—His way.

---

*For more on the fall of Jerusalem and the rebuilding of the wall and gates, read 2 Chronicles 36 and Nehemiah chapters 1-8.

> *"Because thy lovingkindness is better than life,*
> *my lips shall praise thee."*
> —Psalm 63:3

Praise Reveals "The Victim Role"

When life doesn't seem to be going as planned, it is so easy to assume the victim role. You know the victim role. Let's recollect the times when we cried, "I can't do anything right. I feel as though no one cares. I am in this all alone. I just wish that I was dead."

My past work experience was in social services. I provided therapeutic intervention for teenagers who were physically, emotionally, and/or sexually abused by their parent, guardian, or some significant adult. Often these teens would say, "I'm this way because of what my mom did to me." I would respond, "What happened to you in the past was wrong, and part of the healing process is acknowledging the wrong that was done. However, to say that where you are now is because of what happened to you in the past is not accepting responsibility for the decisions you made to arrive at this point. To say, 'I'm here because of what my mom did to me' is to say that you have no control over your life."

When we "play" the victim role with God, we say, "God, I am here because of you." We play the blame game and tell God everything is His fault. We act as though we had no control over our lives. Furthermore, we neglect to accept responsibility for the decisions we made. Actually, when we "play" the victim role, we insinuate that God is not faithful when in fact, I Corinthians 1:9 reads, "God is faithful." Furthermore, Deuteronomy 32:4

reads, "He is the Rock, his work is perfect: for all his ways are judgment: a God of truth and without iniquity, just and right is he." The word "truth" in Deuteronomy 32:4 is translated *emuwnah* and means "fidelity" or "the state of being faithful." Therefore, the verse is saying not only is God a faithful God, "faithful" is how God spiritually exists all the time and, for us, how God operates at any given time.

The victim role deceives. To illustrate this point, I am reminded of the story of Adam and Eve. The end result of the matter is that Eve "saw that the tree was good for food, and that it was pleasant to the eyes, and a tree to be desired to make one wise, she took of the fruit thereof, and did eat, and gave also unto her husband with her; and he did eat" (Genesis 3:6). What prompted Eve to make such a decision? Could it be that she felt neglected by God? Could it be that she felt that Adam spent more time with the animals than with her? No, Eve thought that God did not have her best interest in mind. The Bible says that the serpent was very wise. He said to Eve, "For God doth know that in the day ye eat thereof, then your eyes shall be opened, and ye shall be as gods, knowing good and evil" (Genesis 3:5). What Eve heard, as the serpent lied to

> *Praise nullifies the victim role. Praise places God in the driver's seat and quiets the soul while the will of God is being perfected. The Millionaire Christian refuses to accept the victim role and leans on the love of Christ to overcome all hurt and disappointments.*

her, was that God was holding back. She believed that God was keeping the good part for Himself. Eve justified her actions by believing that she was the victim. God was doing her wrong.

The victim role interferes with our fellowship with God. When we justify our actions by assuming the victim role, we take on a "what about me" attitude. The "what about me" attitude maintains the position that *my feelings* weigh in first, and *my point of view* is more important. I remember when I played the role of the victim and accepted the "what about me" attitude. In 2001, my cousin passed away. My cousin was vibrant and full of life. Do you know someone that is vibrant and full of life? Do you know someone that is always energetic, always smiling, and always has a positive outlook on life? You know, someone you would never expect to suddenly pass away.

I remember traveling from Peoria to Chicago to visit her in the hospital. Her condition was downgraded to critical and her prognosis was not good. My cousin didn't wait for me. She passed away before I arrived. I did not get a chance to say goodbye. I was deeply hurt. I felt as though I was a victim—like something was stolen from me. As I stood by her hospital bed crying, anger started to creep into my heart. I remember telling God, "What about me? I am going to miss my cousin's smile. I am going to miss the one-on-one time that she gave me when I visited with family. I am going to miss the backyard bar-b-que parties when my cousin would be dressed, as the older folks say, 'too sharp' in coordinating colors and accessories from head to toe. What about me, God? What about me?"

The moment I began asking God, "What about me?" my fellowship with Jesus was broken. The same thing happened to James and John when they were traveling with Jesus to Jerusalem.

In Luke 9, Jesus sent messengers to a village of the Samaritans to make arrangements for His arrival. However, the Samaritans did not welcome Jesus. Well, James and John did not like the Samaritans' response, so they asked Jesus, "Lord wilt thou that we command fire to come down from heaven, and consume them, even as Elias did?" (v. 54). The moment this question was asked, fellowship with Jesus was broken.

A fellowship is a partnership. The partnership signifies shared mission, shared goals, and shared outcomes. According to I Corinthians 1:9, "God is faithful. By whom ye were called unto the fellowship of his Son Jesus Christ our Lord." We have a partnership with Jesus Christ. We share Jesus' mission, goals, and outcomes. Therefore, when James and John asked to call fire down from heaven to destroy the Samaritans, Jesus replied, "Ye know not what manner of spirit ye are of. For the Son of man is not come to destroy men's lives, but to save them" (v. 55). Jesus was saying, "That's not the mission, that's not the goal, and that's definitely not the outcome." The disciples broke fellowship and I did, too.

The "what about me" attitude exposed my selfishness and self-centeredness. Here I broke fellowship with Jesus because the love of Christ conquered selfishness and self-centeredness (Romans 12:10). The "what about me" attitude depicted my cousin's passing as the end of her life. Here I broke fellowship with Jesus because we have eternal life (John 3:15). The "what about me" attitude ushered in the victim role. I felt defeated. Here I broke fellowship because I have victory through my Lord Jesus Christ (I Corinthians 15:57).

Praise nullifies the victim role. Praise places God in the driver's seat and quiets the soul while the will of God is being perfected. The Millionaire Christian refuses to accept the victim role and leans on the love of Christ to overcome all hurts and disappointments.

The Millionaire Christian profits from Spiritual Capital.
During challenging times,
Praise
Spiritual agreement with God, remaining steadfast in His will, and depending on the love of Christ
Is
Spiritual Capital

Praise Ye The Lord!

"Praise ye the Lord. Praise God in his sanctuary: praise him in the firmament of his power. Praise him for his mighty acts; praise him according to his excellent greatness. Praise him with the sound of the trumpet: praise him with the psaltery and harp. Praise him with timbrel and dance: praise him with stringed instruments and organs. Praise him upon the loud cymbals: praise him upon the high sounding cymbals. Let everything that hath breath praise the Lord. Praise ye the Lord."

—Psalm 150

> *"Therefore doth my Father love me, because I lay down my life, that I might take it again. No man taketh it from me, but I lay it down of myself. I have power to lay it down, and I have power to take it again. This commandment have I received of my Father."*
> —John 10:17-18

Power

Power Reveals All Possibilities

One of the most powerful scriptures in the Bible is found in Luke 18. A rich ruler came to Jesus and asked, "Good Master, what must I do to inherit eternal life?" (v.18). Jesus responded, "Keep the commandments." The rich ruler responded that he has kept the commandments since he was a youth. Jesus then told him to sell everything he had and to give it to the poor. The rich ruler was very sorrowful, as he was very rich. Jesus continued to say how hard it was for those that have riches to enter into the kingdom of God. Those who heard replied to Jesus, "Who then can be saved?" (v. 26). Jesus responded, "The things which are impossible with men are possible with God" (v. 27).

In 1996, my doctor detected some abnormal growth (via a Pap test) in my cervix. She recommended a conization, or cone biopsy. I consented. A cone biopsy is a medical procedure where tissue, in the shape of a cone, is removed from the cervical area. During the follow-up visit, the doctor shared the results. She told me that much tissue had to be removed. She continued to say that I would suffer miscarriages and/or my cervix would not remain closed should I become pregnant, preventing me from carrying a baby full term. The doctor recommended a hysterectomy. When I heard the word "hysterectomy" my eyes immediately begin to swell with tears. I was only thirty-three years old and it was my prayer to one day marry and have children. In my mind I saw all of my dreams vanish away. I had to regroup, and regroup fast. I looked at her and said, "No. I'm not having a hysterectomy. I believe God for children." I got off the examination table and left the room.

Days turned into months and months into years, but nonetheless I continued to believe that God would bless me to be a wife and a mother. I maintained my position that God was all-powerful and NOTHING was too hard for Him. In March 1999, I married God's best for me. In June of the same year I became pregnant. Now here's the power of God. Not only did I have one child, but God blessed me to give birth to two children, and both pregnancies were FULL term! Is there anything too hard for God?

During challenging times the Millionaire Christian knows that no problem is too big or too hard for God. There's nothing too difficult for Him—nothing at all!

God is not limited by a doctor's report or a surgical procedure. God is great! David said "the heaven and heaven of heavens cannot contain" Him (I Kings 8:27). During challenging times the Millionaire Christian knows that no problem is too big or too hard for God. There's nothing too difficult for Him—nothing at all!

> *"For which cause we faint not; but though our outward man perish, yet the inward man is renewed day by day."*
> —2 Corinthians 4:16

Power

Power Reveals Renewable Energy

The gospel of John records the enlightening conversation between Jesus and Nicodemus. Nicodemus was a member of the Jewish Council. He came to Jesus by night, and Jesus expounded on being "born again." Jesus said to Nicodemus, "The wind bloweth where it listeth, and thou hearest the sound thereof, but canst not tell whence it cometh, and whither it goeth: so is everyone that is born of the Spirit" (John 3:8). Let me ask you a question. Have you ever seen the wind? The correct answer to this question is "no." However, when checking the weather we often say, "It's a windy day," or "The wind is really blowing." In actuality we never see the wind, however, we do see, feel, and hear the effects of the wind.

Simply put, wind is air in motion. Wind is a powerful energy force that makes its presence known. Wind is a renewable energy source. This means that wind is continuously replenished. It never runs out after use. It is restored again and again, again and again, and again and again. So is everyone who is born of the Spirit. The Spirit is a Renewable Energy Source, continuously replenished and never running out after use. And just like the wind, although you cannot see the Spirit, you definitely see the effects.

The Millionaire Christian is power-impacted with the same Spirit that raised Jesus from the dead (Romans 8:11). Therefore, the Millionaire Christian is a renewable energy source. We are constantly doing good deeds, praying without ceasing, and we complete every task that is set before us. The Spirit restores the Millionaire Christian again and again, again and again, and again and again. When we think we cannot endure one moment longer, our spirit says, "Oh yes we can! Oh yes we can!"

The Millionaire Christian profits from Spiritual Capital. During challenging times,
Power
Knowing that with God everything is possible and nothing is impossible for the Spirit restores over and over, and over again
Is
Spiritual Capital

REVIEW QUESTIONS

Prayer Reveals The Source

1. Prayer is our Christian _____.

2. God is the ____ ____ ____ ____ ____ ____.

3. Explain how God is your Source. _____
   _____
   _____

4. The _____ is dangerous living.

5. Recall a time when you lived in the "comfort zone." What did you rely upon?
   _____
   _____

6. Prayer is a spirit d _____. Which means:

7. Why would people prefer to live in the comfort zone?
   _____
   _____

Prayer Reveals Expectancy

1. Prayer has _____.

2. What does expectancy mean to you?

   _____

   _____

   _____

   _____

3. Considering your prayer request(s), what are your expectations from God?

   _____

   _____

   _____

4. Explain what you think happens to our spirits when there is no expectation from God.

   _____

   _____

   _____

Prayer-Praise-Power Is Spiritual Capital

Praise Reveals Agreement With God

1. Psalm 22 is referred to as the Psalm of the _____

2. Write about a time when you felt "forsaken." Explain how you restored agreement with God. _____

   _____

3. Praise keeps us in _____ with God.

4. Praise is our spiritual gauge used to _____, _____, and _____ spiritual agreement with God.

5. Rebekah said to God, "If you have answered my prayer, then why is my life like this?" Explain how you identify with her statement. _____

   _____

Praise Reveals No Compromises

1. Praise leaves no room for _____.

2. Write about a time when you praised God:

   _____

   _____

The Millionaire Christian

3. When the enemy tried to stop Nehemiah from rebuilding the wall, Nehemiah measured the enemy's word against the _____ of _____ and knew that God did not send them.

4. Write about a time when you compromised the will of God:

   _____

   _____

Praise Reveals "The Victim Role"

1. In your own words, explain the victim role. _____

2. I played the "victim role" when: _____

   _____

3. The Millionaire Christian praises God because the Millionaire Christian knows God is f_____.

4. The victim role d _____.

5. Write five things you praise God for:

   a. _____

   b. _____

   c. _____

Prayer-Praise-Power Is Spiritual Capital

   d. _____

   e. _____

6. The victim role interferes with our _____ with God.

7. Write about a time when you conquered the "what about me" attitude. _____
_____

8. A fellowship is a _____.

9. Praise _____ the victim role.

10. A partnership shares the same _____, _____, and _____

Power Reveals All Possibilities

1. Things that are _____ for men are _____ with God (Luke 18:27).

2. Nothing is too _____ for God.

3. Write about a time when God made the impossible possible for you: _____
_____
_____

Power Reveals Renewable Energy

1. The Spirit r____ ____ ____ ____ ____ ____ ____ the Millionaire Christian.

2. The Spirit is a renewable _____ source.

3. When you think you cannot endure one moment longer, your spirit says, _____
   _____

Take a moment and journal to God your thoughts, revelations, or reflections received from reading this Key Attribute.

Reflection: _____
_____
_____
_____
_____

KEY ATTRIBUTE 2

Commitment Is Spiritual Capital

"If a man die, shall he live again? All the days of my appointed time will I wait, till my change come."
—Job 14:14

Commitment

DURING CHALLENGING TIMES, we petition God for answers and we ask ourselves stimulating questions. For example, "Did I make the right decision?" and "Why is this happening to me?" We begin to contemplate what actions we need to take in order to relieve ourselves of the misery and pain. When pondering our choices for relief, be it known that suicide is not an option. Sometimes life can go from bad to worse. We feel as though all doors of opportunities have been closed shut and the only viable escape is death. Our desire is for immediate relief. Our thinking becomes, what better immediate relief than a greater pain to eliminate the existing pain? Sounds foolish?

Oh no, this is the mind of those who attempt suicide. They just want to the pain to stop.

What choices do you make when day-to-day living becomes a hard thing to do? Hard things are beyond our capability to impact, influence, and change. For example, Elijah faced a hard thing. In 2 Kings 2, Elijah was on his journey to be received by God. His servant Elisha was traveling close by his side. "And it came to pass, when they were gone over, that Elijah said unto Elisha, Ask what I shall do for thee, before I be taken away from thee. And Elisha said, I pray thee, let a double portion of thy spirit be upon me." Elijah responded, "Thou has asked a hard thing" (v. 9-10). The spirit that Elijah had was not his spirit. It was God's Spirit. Elisha asked Elijah to do something that Elijah didn't even do for himself. Elijah was saying, *Wow, I can't give you a double of something that I did not manufacture. Heck, it was given to me. That's a hard thing.* A hard thing is a God thing. A hard thing is something that we cannot do or give; only God can do it and only God can give it.

During these tough economic times, many people are faced with a hard thing. Many people have looked at their situation and declared it hopeless. Some have resolved within themselves that the only thing keeping them alive is their commitment to God. The words "*I belong to God. I belong to God*" resound in their spirit and keeps them focused just long enough to overcome each challenge—day by day. Our commitment to God can be the deciding factor between claiming victory and accepting defeat. Commitment is a conscious, voluntary decision confirmed by a series of actions that set apart, surrender, and bond, our entire being (mind, body, spirit and soul).

Commitment Is Spiritual Capital

Commitment was the deciding factor in the transference of power between Elijah and Elisha. Elisha asked for a double portion of Elijah's spirit. Elijah responded, "If thou see me when I am taken from thee, it shall be so unto thee; but if not, it shall not be so" (v.10). Paraphrasing, Elijah was saying, "Elisha, receiving a double portion of the spirit that rests upon me is between you and God. What I do know is that if you are committed to God, He will answer your request. If you are not committed, it will not be so." Elisha was committed. He refused to allow anything or anyone to hinder, distract, or block his focus, purpose, and mission. Elisha was so committed that the chariot of fire had to separate him from Elijah—"And it came to pass, as they still went on, and talked, that, behold, *there appeared* a chariot of fire, and horses of fire, and parted them both asunder; and Elijah went up by a whirlwind into heaven" (2 Kings 2:11).

The Millionaire Christian has made a voluntary decision to set apart, surrender, and bond their entire being to God through Jesus Christ. When the pressure mounts and people try to block their breakthrough and deliverance, the Millionaire Christian confirms their commitment and presses through the opposition until they encounter Jesus.

To be committed means to finish. No matter how difficult the situation may appear to be, we finish—we let life run its course. Jesus is our greatest example to reference when it comes to finishing hard things. Jesus was committed to God even to the point of dying on the cross. When hard things appear to be hopeless things and we feel like quitting before God's appointed time, we reference Jesus and we brand in our spirit Hebrews 12:2-3. The scripture reads:

> "Looking unto Jesus the author and finisher of our faith; who for the joy that was set before him endured the cross, despising the shame, and is set down at the right hand of the throne of God. For consider him that endured such contradiction of sinners against himself, lest ye be wearied and faint in your minds."

Commitment guarantees our breakthrough. For example, Blind Bartimaeus was a beggar that sat by the roadside. As people passed by, he petitioned them for support. When he heard a loud gathering, he inquired to find out what was going on. Blind Bartimaeus was told that Jesus was passing by. "And when he heard that it was Jesus of Nazareth, he began to cry out, and say, Jesus, Son of David have mercy on me" (Mark 10:47). It's important to note that when Blind Bartimaeus heard that Jesus was passing by, he cried out, "Jesus, thou Son of David." The title "Son of David" is the name for the Messiah, the Anointed One, the Christ.

Being blind, Bartimaeus could not see with his natural eyes. Nonetheless, Bartimaeus was committed to the belief that Jesus possessed the power to restore his sight. In fact, Bartimaeus was so committed that when he shouted for Jesus and many commanded him to be quiet, he cried out even more—a great deal more. The crowd was cheering as if some famous celebrity was passing by, but not Bartimaeus. Although he could not see with his natural eyes, Bartimaeus saw more in Jesus than sighted man could see. He knew that the Messiah, the Anointed One, the Christ was passing by.

The Millionaire Christian has made a voluntary decision to set apart, surrender, and bond their entire being to God through Jesus Christ. When the pressure mounts and people try to block their breakthrough and deliverance, the Millionaire Christian confirms their commitment and presses through the opposition until they encounter Jesus.

The Millionaire Christian profits from Spiritual Capital.
During challenging times,
Commitment
Finishing the course of life that is set before us
Is
Spiritual Capital

Review Questions

1. _____ is not an option.

2. Hard things are beyond our limit to _____, _____, and _____.

3. A hard thing is a _____ thing.

4. What "hard thing" are you currently facing or have faced? How is/was God involved? _____
   _____

5. What is the definition of commitment? _____
   _____
   _____

6. To be committed means to f_____.

7. In your own words, explain why the crowd cheered as if a celebrity was passing by but Blind Bartimaeus cried, "Jesus, Son of David, have mercy on me."
   _____
   _____

8. Commitment _____ our breakthrough.

Commitment Is Spiritual Capital

9. The Millionaire Christian has made a _____ decision to _____, _____, and _____ their entire being to God.

10. What steps do you need to take (be it spiritual, mental, or physical) to ensure that you will finish? _____

_____

Take a moment and journal to God your thoughts, revelations, or reflections received from reading this Key Attribute.

Reflection: _____

_____

_____

_____

_____

KEY ATTRIBUTE 3

Contentment Is Spiritual Capital

"But godliness with contentment is great gain."
—I Timothy 6:6

Contentment

CHALLENGING TIMES CAN make us lose touch with reality. We feel as though our life is a dramatic movie—so many issues and continuous conflicts. With no control over the remote, there are times when we feel as though we are stuck in the rewind mode. Life consists of much repeated drama—we can't win for losing and we often wonder if God is punishing us. On the other hand, there are times when we feel as though we are in the "fast forward" mode—we are ever doing and never receiving. While in this mode, we often wonder if God is pressing the skip button—if He's holding back and refusing to release what we think we have earned or deserve. Finally, challenging times can make us feel as though our life is in the "pause mode." Nothing is happening. We are not winning or losing. We are just waiting, and waiting, and waiting. Life appears to be at a standstill and we are anxiously waiting for God to press the play button.

Challenging times can make us feel as though we are twisted and turned, pushed and pulled, and beaten and battered. How do we make sense of it all? How do we win our emotional wars without positioning God as the enemy? There's no better person to reference when seeking answers to these questions than the Apostle Paul. Paul's life demonstrated that contentment provides the balance to living an enjoyable life in harmony with God.

Paul was no stranger to challenging times. "Of the Jews five times received I forty stripes save one. Thrice was I beaten with rods, once was I stoned, thrice I suffered shipwreck, a night and a day I have been in the deep; in journeying often, in perils of waters, in perils of robbers, in perils by my own countrymen, in perils by the heathen, in perils in the city, in perils in the wilderness, in perils in the sea, in perils among false brethren; in weariness and painfulness, in watching often, in hunger and thirst, in fastings often, in cold and nakedness" (2 Corinthians 11:24-27). Yet, despite the challenges he faced, Paul commented that he learned to be content in whatsoever state (Philippians 4:11).

> *The Millionaire Christian lives a life of contentment.*

Paul learned contentment. He said that in whatsoever stage of persecution he was facing, he was content. What was Paul actually saying? What is contentment? Is it walking around with your head held high, projecting to people that you have no struggles? Before I got married, people would say to me, "God will send you a mate once you get "content" with yourself." I thought I was "content." I began to think, *What do they know that I don't know?* Then one day God spoke to me and said, "Do you know why you are not married?" I answered, "No, God." He said, "If you were married and someone asked you, 'What did you do to get your mate?' you would proceed to tell them everything you did and the steps you took to get a mate. You would highlight your achievements and merits and take all the credit, when in fact, it was nothing you did to get the mate. You received the mate because of who I am and because of my faithfulness." This conversation with God led me to question my motives. Was I serving God because He is God or was I serving God based on what I wanted from Him? I asked myself, "How would you feel if you never married?" Was I really content or was I merely living to be satisfied?

When Paul said that he learned to be content, he was saying that his position and his point of view was that in every situation, not only did he have what he needed, he had how much he needed. One trick of the enemy is to make Christians believe that no matter how much they receive, it is never enough. Over time, personal satisfaction becomes the primary focus. Paul's primary focus was to do God's will. His focus was not personal satisfaction. Therefore, Paul believed that God would supply him with what he needed and how much he needed to do His will. So, if he did not have it, Paul knew that he didn't need it.

There is a difference between seeking personal satisfaction and being content with God's will. Seeking personal satisfaction is an insult to God. This I had to learn first hand. I remember one night my husband and I were flicking through the channels trying to find something to watch on television. He stopped at a channel that was advertising 1970's music. He and I began to reminisce about the "old days" and I began to think about how good those days were. To be honest, in my heart I began to miss those days and I began to long for those days to come back once more. Do you know what I'm talking about? Have you ever longed for those "good old days" when you were much younger and life wasn't as complicated—as though those past days were better than the days you're now living? Well, after this experience, I read Ecclesiastes 7:10—"Say not thou, What is the cause that the former days were better than these? For thou dost not inquire wisely concerning this." Paraphrasing, the scripture is saying, don't say that the old days, the days of the past were better than the days of the present. To say this is not wise. Why? God ministered to me that when I longed for the days of the past, I was actually saying that God treated me better then than He does now. Longing for those "good old days" was a discredit to His goodness, His grace, His kindness, and His mercy shown to me throughout the years and up to the present day. In other words, I was indirectly asking God, "What have you done for me lately?" To long for the days of the past as if those days were better than the present is directly related to personal satisfaction. I had to accept the fact that when I thought I was content, I was only living to be satisfied.

When we are content, our relationship with God is based on who God is. When we seek personal satisfaction, our relationship with God is based on what He can do. The Millionaire Christian lives a life of contentment. The Millionaire Christian, like Paul, lives as though God has supplied them with what they need to do His will. So if there's something they don't have, the Millionaire Christian believes they don't need it. Ask yourself, are you content or are you merely living to be satisfied?

The Millionaire Christian profits from Spiritual Capital.
During challenging times,
Contentment
Knowing that God has provided what you need and how much you need
Is
Spiritual Capital

REVIEW QUESTIONS

1. Is your life in the "rewind mode," the "fast forward mode," or the "pause mode"?

   Explain why: _____

   _____

2. Paul's primary focus _____.

3. Paul's point of view was that God gave him _____ he needed and _____ much he needed.

4. Seeking _____ is an insult to God.

5. When we are content, our relationship with God is based on who God _____. When we seek personal satisfaction, our relationship with God is based on what He _____.

6. Finish this sentence: I believe that God has supplied me with everything I need to do His will. So if there's something I don't have, then I believe I don't _____.

7. Before reading this Attribute, were you content or were you seeking personal satisfaction? Explain your answer:

   _____

   _____

   _____

Contentment Is Spiritual Capital

Take a moment and journal to God your thoughts, revelations, or reflections received from reading this Key Attribute.

Reflection: _____

_____

_____

_____

_____

KEY ATTRIBUTE 4

Confidence Is Spiritual Capital

*"For the Lord shall be thy confidence,
and shall keep thy foot from being taken."*
—Proverbs 3:26

Confidence

THERE'S NO BETTER display of confidence than the confidence displayed by King Hezekiah. Hezekiah was the son of King Ahaz, the King of Judah. Hezekiah was twenty-five years old when he inherited the throne, and he reigned for approximately twenty-nine years. Hezekiah removed and destroyed principles and practices that were contrary to God's will and God's way. The Bible says that he was a king that "did that which was right in the sight of the Lord, according to all that David his father did" (2 Kings 18:3). Hezekiah removed high places, broke down sacred pillars, and kept God's commandments. More importantly, he refused to serve the king of Assyria. Hezekiah clung to the Lord and trusted in his God.

In the fourteenth year of Hezekiah's reign, Sennacherib, king of Assyria, attacked Judah and captured the fortified cities. Sennacherib sent messengers to inform the people that Hezekiah was misleading them and lying to them. One of the messengers, Rabshakeh, said, "But if ye say unto me, We trust in the Lord our God: is not that he, whose high places and whose altars Hezekiah hath taken away, and hath said to Judah and Jerusalem, Ye shall worship before this altar in Jerusalem?" (2 Kings 18:22). These words traveled fast to Hezekiah and when he heard, he tore his clothes, and covered himself with sackcloth (a public display of his emotional state), and went into the house of the Lord. When the king of Assyria saw that King Hezekiah neither surrendered nor retaliated, he sent yet another report, but this time in writing. "And Hezekiah received the letter of the hand of the messengers, and read it: and Hezekiah went up into the house of the Lord, and spread it before the Lord" (2 Kings 19:14).

> *Confidence requires the setting of boundaries, walls to divide the acceptable from the unacceptable. Such boundaries mirror our tolerance and set the stage for God to come to our defense. A Millionaire Christian sets boundaries.*

Hezekiah was at a moment of truth. For about fourteen years prior to inheriting the throne, Hezekiah ruled alongside of his father. Hezekiah's father ruled not after God's will or God's way. Despite living under, witnessing, and being subjected to the negative things his father did, Hezekiah believed God. Hezekiah was so radical for God that in the beginning of his reign, he rebelled against the king of Assyria and stopped paying the tribute that was imposed when his father was king. The king of Assyria thought he had Hezekiah on the old ball and chain. You know the saying "Like father, like son." Hezekiah's revolt baffled the king of Assyria, and he asked, "On what are you basing this confidence?" The king of Assyria saw all of Hezekiah's reforms and asked, "Who do you think you are? Or better yet, whose do you think you are?"

> "And Hezekiah prayed before the Lord, and said, O Lord God of Israel, which dwellest between the cherubims, thou art the God, even thou alone, of all the kingdoms of the earth; thou hast made heaven and earth. Lord, bow down thine ear, and hear: open, Lord, thine eyes, and see: and hear the words of Sennacherib, which hath made heaven and earth. Lord, bow down thine ear, and hear: open Lord, thine eyes, and see: and hear the words of Sennacherib, which hath sent him to reproach the living God, Of truth, Lord, the kings of Assyria have destroyed the nations and their lands, And have cast their gods into the fire: for they were no gods, but the work of men's hands, wood and stone: therefore they have destroyed them. Now therefore, O Lord our God, I beseech thee, save thou us out of his hand, and all the kingdoms of the earth may know that thou art the Lord God, even thou only."
> —2 Kings 19:15-19

Hezekiah placed confidence in God and trusted God to do what He said He would do. Now an interesting point needs to be made here. Although trust and confidence go hand-in-hand, the two are very different. It is possible to trust someone but have no confidence in them. Also, it is possible to have confidence in someone but not trust them. This is because trust is based on character and confidence is based on ability. For example, your sixteen-year-old wants to stay at home while you travel out of town for the weekend. You are confident that she is able to stay at home by herself and that she would take care of herself as well as the house. However, you do not trust that she would make the right decisions while you are gone. Confidence is us saying to God, "God, you can do this." Trust is God saying to us, "Know that I can do this."

Hezekiah's confidence said, "God is able." Hezekiah's trust said, "God will answer," and He did.

> "And it came to pass that night, that the angel of the Lord went out, and smote in the camp of the Assyrians an hundred fourscore and five thousand: and when they arose early in the morning, behold, they were all dead corpses. So Sennacherib king of Assyria departed, and went and returned, and dwelt at Nineveh."
>
> —2 Kings 19:35-36

Confidence leaves no room for compromise. There was no agreement between King Hezekiah and King Sennacherib. Sennacherib wanted Hezekiah to serve him, but Hezekiah stood fast and maintained his service to God. Sennacherib tried to manipulate Hezekiah into surrendering. However, Hezekiah set boundaries and refused to surrender.

Confidence requires the setting of boundaries, walls to divide the acceptable from the unacceptable. Such boundaries mirror our tolerance and set the stage for God to come to our defense.

The Millionaire Christian sets boundaries. The Millionaire Christian's boundaries affirm and announce God's principles and standards as the determining factor for how they allow others to treat them. Setting boundaries is not issuing a threat or trying to manipulate the enemy. On the contrary, by setting boundaries the Millionaire Christian has determined and has declared to make no agreement with the enemy. The Millionaire Christian knows that God possesses the means, resources, and power to perform whatever needs to be done.

The Millionaire Christian profits from Spiritual Capital.
During challenging times,
Confidence
Knowing God is able
Is
Spiritual Capital

Review Questions

1. Trust is based on _____.

2. Confidence is based on _____.

3. Using a personal life experience, write about a time when you trusted someone and when you had confidence in someone. Explain the difference. _____

   _____

   _____

   _____

4. Confidence stores no room for _____.

5. Confidence requires the setting of _____.

6. Explain a boundary you have set in your life with each of the following. Be specific—name who and what boundary.

   a. With a family member: _____

   _____

   b. With a member of the opposite gender: _____

   _____

   c. With a co-worker: _____

   _____

Confidence Is Spiritual Capital

Take a moment and journal to God your thoughts, revelations, or reflections received from reading this Key Attribute.

Reflection: _____

_____

_____

_____

KEY ATTRIBUTE 5

Self-Forgiveness Is Spiritual Capital

"I acknowledged my sin unto thee, and mine iniquity have I not hid. I said, I will confess my transgressions unto the Lord; and thou forgavest the iniquity of my sin."
—Psalm 32:5

Self-Forgiveness

CHALLENGING TIMES CAN spur conflict and controversy that result in emotional wounds. When the challenge is over, recovery and healing begins. However, recovery and healing requires self-forgiveness.

Self-forgiveness means to pardon—to release ourselves from punishment and/or penalty. Self-forgiveness includes erasing the wrongdoing—treating ourselves as if it never happened, and removing the wrongdoing—suppressing all recollection of the wrongdoing ever happening. A third component related to self-forgiveness is silencing our pain associated to the hurt.

Many times it is not our inability to forgive others that hinders emotional recovery and healing; it is the inability to forgive ourselves. The inability to forgive ourselves is the result of holding our emotions captive. When we experience hurt feelings, it is a reflexive response to either retaliate or withdraw. Retaliation is an expression of our emotions. However, when we withdraw we shelter our emotions—hold our emotions captive. The intent behind sheltered emotions is to prevent further hurt. When emotional healing begins, sheltered emotions aren't filtered through the healing process. Sheltered emotions are protected emotions and protected emotions are wounded emotions and wounded emotions can not forgive.

When we fail to forgive ourselves, our pain becomes a messenger to alert our emotions of potential threats. We depend on the pain to analyze and interpret whether a situation is safe or unsafe. The problem with this is that pain attracts pain. Therefore, when we fail to forgive ourselves, our pain sends a signal to our emotions, and our emotions classify every person and every situation as unsafe or a potential threat. In order to protect ourselves while simultaneously interacting within our social context, we group everybody into one big category—*everyone is out to hurt me*. So no matter what relationship we enter into or

> *To the Millionaire Christian, self-forgiveness is debt cancellation. Self-forgiveness mirrors the same debt cancellation received through the birth, death, and resurrection of Jesus Christ.*

what situation we find ourselves in, we wait for and even expect the pain to come.

When we fail to forgive ourselves, we depict everyone as the enemy. We cope with reality by responding defensively in our behavior and communication. In order to protect ourselves, we set conditions—standards for people to meet before gaining our trust. We believe in "false truths," meaning that we are always right and everyone else is always wrong. Our expectations for all of our relationships are clearly communicated and defined. The bottom line is that we make people feel as though they are walking on eggshells, meaning that in order to prevent an explosive moment, they always have to be careful what they say and what they do.

Seven Paths To Self-Forgiveness

Self-forgiveness is debt cancellation. Self-forgiveness mirrors the same debt cancellation received through the birth, death, and resurrection of Jesus Christ. Following are seven paths to self-forgiveness. The first five are:

#1. We acknowledge the wrongful act—we refuse to live a life of regrets. We confess our faults and invite prayers for our healing (James 5:16).

#2. We pardon those who have hurt us. We stop trying to get even and we make a decision to love (Matthew 6:12).

#3. We trust God. We depend on God to make things happen (Psalm 118:8).

#4. We live in the present, thereby canceling feelings of anger and resentment (Matthew 6:11).

#5. We transform (Romans 12:2).

How is it that we can close our eyes and see that one moment in time when pain was introduced in to our lives? Although years and years have passed, the pain penetrates like a fresh wound, as if it happened yesterday. Moreover, if we focus on the pain long enough, we have to quickly turn our heads or suddenly open our eyes to stop the tears from flowing. When it comes to our past, we are a bowl of emotions, and at times we feel as though we are being whipped, stirred, and mixed. Our emotions are so toggled that we don't know if we should laugh or cry. Therefore, we resolve in our minds, "I won't let anyone see my pain," believing that we can alter our emotions by refusing to feel the pain. Not true. What we fail to realize is that emotions are not feelings, and vice versa: feelings are not emotions. Feelings are connected to our senses, and emotions are connected to our thinking. So the solution now becomes not changing the way we feel in order to stop the pain. The correct response is changing the way we think in order to stop the pain. The bottom line: the mind must be renewed. A spiritual transformation must take place.

An example of feelings and emotions is when a child reaches out to touch fire. The fire burns and the senses (the feelings) process the touch as pain. The child withdraws his/her hand and immediately the mind is branded with the thinking that "fire hurts"—the emotions. The next time the child sees fire, without feeling the sensation of pain, the child will resort to his/her emotions and think, "Fire hurts." Christians battling emotional pain do this all the time. They attach and generalize their emotions, their thinking from past experiences, to their present situation.

For example, if Daddy was the one that caused the pain, the Christian will generalize her emotions to every man she meets.

Her thinking becomes, "Men are no good" and "All men cause pain." Now although this particular Christian may not audibly say these things or rehearse the statements in her mind, her actions and reactions will definitely project her emotions. In addition, should intimacy increase, out of fear that pain will follow or the joy experienced is too good to be true (because in her mind, men are no good), she will resort to her emotions and immediately end the relationship. Soon after, this Christian is left wondering why every relationship has been unsuccessful; why every man she meets does, in fact, hurt her. Why is she still single? Or maybe she thought that marriage would make her happy and heal every pain in her life. However, even though she's married, she's still not happy. She experiences no joy and if the truth be told, she would rather go back to being single. Why? It is because she failed to renew her mind. She was not transformed, so she conformed to her emotions. Therefore her emotions branded her thinking, her thinking developed her character, her character influenced her decisions, and her decisions determined the outcome.

Romans 12:2 reads: "And be not conformed to this world: but be ye transformed by the renewing of your mind, that ye may prove what is that good, and acceptable, and perfect, will of God." The word "renewing" is *anakainosis* in the Greek. *Anakainosis* means restoration. It is through the renewing process that a broken and damaged spirit is restored. The process of renewing replaces painful memories with inspiring encounters with Christ. As scripture is embedded in our spirit via reading and studying the word of God, deep-rooted thinking attached to the pain is extracted. Our thoughts originate from a new mind—the mind of Christ. Our character is no longer the product of a painful past but is transformed and aligned with the perfect character of Jesus Christ.

The second part of the renewing process is proving the good, acceptable, and perfect will of God. The word "prove" is *dokimazo* in the Greek, and it means "to test." The prerequisite for testing that good, acceptable, and perfect will of God is founded on knowing and internalizing God's word. Bible scholars presume that Psalm 119 is the work of King David. If so, David internalized God's word when he "hid" God's word in his heart (Psalm 119:11). The word "hid" in this verse means to hoard, to store for future use. David was a military man. As a military man, he had to make sure every part of him that could be an entry for sin was protected and entrenched in God's word. Then, in the advent he might have overlooked an entry point, a possibility, David told God, "I have hid your word in my heart." In other words, David told God, "God, while I am serving as king, should sin come and entice me, I have stored an extra supply of your word in my heart so that I won't sin against you."

We too must hide God's word in our heart. We must hoard and claim in the spirit realm just like we would hoard and claim in the natural. For example, maybe you've done this before—you're shopping when you see the last shirt or blouse on the rack, the only one in your size. Without thinking, you grab it. As you proceed to the checkout, you realize you don't have enough money to buy the blouse. Nonetheless you claim the blouse as "your blouse." So you take the blouse and hide it—you camouflage the blouse between other clothes on the rack. You hoard the blouse—you store it until you can return to purchase it. You hid the blouse because you did not want any one else to buy it. In addition, by hiding the blouse you preserved the blouse—you made it nonexistent and blocked buyers from purchasing the blouse. In doing so, you kept the blouse available and accessible only to you.

Hiding the blouse on the rack mirrors the same intent that David spoke of when he said he "hid" God's word in his heart. David's heart is that blouse. David took his heart and camouflaged it with God's word. David hoarded God's word in his heart just like the blouse was hoarded on the rack of clothes. He made his heart difficult for the world to find. In addition, he blocked the world's attempt to capture his heart and tempt him to sin. Furthermore, David's heart was available and accessible only to God. Hiding God's word in his heart transformed David. His mind was renewed and able to test that good, acceptable, and perfect will of God.

Proving the good, acceptable, and perfect will of God distinguishes us from those conformed to the world. The world does not dictate or control our emotions. The world does not brand our thinking. Our minds have been renewed and we define what is good. We define what is acceptable. We define what is perfect. We have the character of Christ. Transformation is a prerequisite for self-forgiveness. The world might struggle with self-forgiveness, but we don't. We have been transformed and we forgive because we have been forgiven.

The remaining two paths to self-forgiveness are:

- **#6.** We value the blessings bestowed upon us. We appreciate and count special the people and possessions God has given us (Ecclesiastes 5:18).
- **#7.** We see forgiveness as granting "new beginnings" and not giving "second chances."

When petitioning God for forgiveness, it has been said that God gives second chances. Therefore, when seeking forgiveness, some Christians ask God for a second chance. Little is it realized that when seeking a second chance, the first chance (which is attached to the past) has to remain first—there must be a first rank in order to have something ranked as second. However, II Corinthians 5:17 reads: "Therefore if any man be in Christ he is a new creature: old things are passed away; behold all things are become new." The word "new" is *kainos* in the Greek. It means "superior in quality." The scripture is referring to the spiritual rebirth of the inward man resulting from our relationship with Jesus Christ. We didn't get a "second chance" when we accepted Jesus Christ. We received a fresh start. We became new! Also, accepting Jesus Christ moved us to a higher level of existence. We spiritually exist with Christ. Thus, we became superior in quality! Earnest self-forgiveness does not result from receiving second chances. Earnest self-forgiveness results from receiving new beginnings.

New beginnings position the Millionaire Christian to forget what lies behind and to reach forward to what lies ahead. The Millionaire Christian presses toward the goal for the prize of the high calling of God in Christ Jesus (Philippians 3:13-14).

The Millionaire Christian profits from Spiritual Capital.
During challenging times,
Self-forgiveness
Releasing and Erasing wrongdoing
Is
Spiritual Capital

Self-Forgiveness Is Spiritual Capital

REVIEW QUESTIONS

1. Self-forgiveness means to: _____.

2. What is the third component of self-forgiveness?

   _____

   _____.

3. The biggest hindrance to emotional recovery and healing is the _____ to _____ ourselves.

4. The inability to forgive ourselves results from what?

   _____

   _____

5. How do we hold our emotions captive? _____

   _____

6. Write about a time when you sheltered your emotions, held your emotions captive, and could not forgive yourself.

   _____

   _____

7. _____ is an expression of our emotions.

8. Wounded emotions cannot _____.

9. Pain _____ pain.

10. How do you respond when meeting new people? Do you put up a shield of defense as if that person's goal is to hurt you? Explain your answer: _____

_____

_____

11. Self-forgiveness is debt _____.

12. Do you know someone who makes you feel as though you're walking on eggshells? If yes, explain how. _____

_____

13. Discuss how three of the seven ways to self-forgiveness has made an impact on your life. _____

_____

14. Feelings are connected to our _____.

15. Emotions are connected to our _____.

16. Are your emotions tied to your past? If so, how?

_____

_____

17. The process of renewing _____ painful memories with _____ encounters with Christ.

Self-Forgiveness Is Spiritual Capital

18. David _____ God's word in his heart (Psalm 119:11).

19. The word "hid" means to _____ to _____ for _____ use.

20. Hiding God's word in his heart made David's heart _____ for the world to find.

21. Because our mind has been renewed, we define what is _____. We define what is _____. We define what is _____.

22. In your own words, explain the difference between receiving a second chance and a new beginning. _____ _____

23. Write Philippians 3:13-14: _____

Take a moment and journal to God your thoughts, revelations, or reflections received from reading this Key Attribute.

Reflection: _____

_____

_____

_____

_____

KEY ATTRIBUTE 6

Vision Is Spiritual Capital

*"For the vision is yet for an appointed time,
but at the end it shall speak, and not lie: though it tarry,
wait for it; because it will surely come, it will not tarry."*
—Habakkuk 2:3

Vision

IMAGINE YOURSELF SEEKING employment. As job seekers, we approach employment through the eyes of the "applicant." However businesses approach employment through the eyes of the "employer." Even though not employed with the business, the applicant must communicate their skill not as an applicant but as an employee. The applicant must have vision. Vision looks like this:

> Good morning, team! I have good news. Let us take time to congratulate Geneva and welcome her to the team. It's

been a long five months and finally we filled the position. We received 150 resumes for the position. We eliminated 82 resumes because they did not have a cover letter. Of the 68, we eliminated 35 because they did not include a salary history. Of the 33, we shredded 23 because references were not included. The 10 remaining candidates were interviewed for the position. We immediately said no to the first three as they were four to five minutes late. Three of the remaining candidates came to the interview dressed in jeans, and one wore perfume that was so strong her scent arrived before she did. We could only tolerate five minutes of being in the same room with her. Okay, so we were down to our last three candidates. The interviews were going well until we asked one specific question. We asked all of the candidates, "Considering your gifts and your expertise that you bring to the table, what will our business look like three years from now?" The first person said that it depended on the tools the business provided to help "accentuate" his gifts. After we kindly finished laughing, we escorted him to the door and said, "We will call you." The second candidate said that it depended on the world's condition and began to tell us all about the recession the world is experiencing. Again, we escorted her to the door and said, "We will call you." The third candidate, Geneva, was the only one with an outstanding answer. Again we asked, "Considering your gifts and your expertise that you bring to the table, what will our business look like three years from now?" Geneva sat there for a moment with her head down. Suddenly she looked up at us, made eye contact, and said, "I see us inspiring, energizing, and captivating our target market."

What a remarkable answer. Immediately we could see that Geneva was a woman with vision and we quickly offered her the position.

Let me ask you a question: considering your spiritual gifts, what will God's business look like three years from now? I hear you say, "What business?" Do you not know that God has a business? In Luke 2, Jesus was twelve years old, and his parents went to Jerusalem as they did every year for the Feast of the Passover. After traveling for a day, it was discovered that Jesus was not among the family, so they returned to Jerusalem to look for him. After a three-day search, they found Jesus in the temple courts sitting among the teachers, listening to them and asking questions. Mary was very upset: "And when they saw him, they were amazed: and his mother said unto him, Son, why hast thou thus dealt with us? behold, thy father and I have sought thee sorrowing" (v. 48). Jesus responded, "How is it that ye sought me? Wist ye not that I must be about my Father's business?" (Luke 2:49).

The Millionaire Christian is a Christian with vision. Vision positions the Millionaire Christian to triumph all the time and every time.

God has a business. A business is a legal entity that provides some type of goods or services. God's business—His goods and services—are reconciliation and redemption. God made His business legal (and actually legalized us as co-owners) through the birth, death, and resurrection of His Son Jesus Christ. In addition to a business, God has a vision. Businesses refer to vision as branding the future in the present. The vision for God's business is declaring the end in the beginning. God calls those things that are not as though they were (Romans 4:17).

A well-noted vision scripture is Proverbs 29:18: "Where there is no vision, the people perish." The scripture is saying that when we do not see God's intended end in the beginning, we expose ourselves. We stand naked before the enemy and we make ourselves easy targets for attacks. Our failure to declare God's intended end in the beginning drains us of the spiritual strength needed to look beyond our challenging moment. Our day-to-day living becomes so twisted that at times it appears as though we're moving backwards instead of forward. We become stagnated, indecisive, and hopeless. We look at the challenge and declare like Jehoshaphat, "I have no strength to stand." Remember Jehoshaphat king of Judah. He was a king that "did right in the eyes of the Lord," meaning that he followed after God's command. In 2 Chronicles 20, Moab, Ammon, and some of the Meunites came against Jehoshaphat to battle. Some came and told Jehoshaphat, "There cometh a great multitude against thee from beyond the sea on this side Syria; and behold, they be in Hazazon-tamar, which is Engedi" (2 Chronicles 20:2). The next verse reads that "Jehoshaphat feared" (v. 3). Jehoshaphat could not declare God's intended end in the beginning. He did not have vision to look beyond the multitude coming against him and see the victory that God intended. Jehoshaphat prayed, "O our God, wilt thou not judge them? For we have no might against this great company that cometh against us; neither know we what to do: but our eyes are upon thee" (2 Chronicles 20:12).

Vision Is Spiritual Capital

Like Jehoshaphat, the lack of vision leaves us with no strength and no direction. We become feeble and we whine to God, "Make them stop. Make them leave me alone." We become fixated on our challenge and we fail to see the options and opportunities that God is trying to reveal. We render ourselves spiritually useless and ineffective. All the while we wait for God to rescue us—and all the while we perish. Yes, we perish.

Shadrach, Meshach, and Abednego were men with vision. When mandated by Nebuchadnezzar to fall down and worship the golden image, they responded: "O Nebuchadnezzar, we are not careful to answer thee in this matter. If it be so, our God whom we serve is able to deliver us from the burning fiery furnace, and he will deliver us out of thine hand, O king" (Daniel 3:16-17). They saw God's intended end in the beginning. God will deliver! The Millionaire Christian is a Christian with vision, who declares God's intended end in the beginning. The Millionaire Christian sees every challenge just like Shadrach, Meshach, and Abednego saw their challenge—God will deliver! Vision positions the Millionaire Christian to triumph all the time and every time.

> The Millionaire Christian profits from Spiritual Capital.
> During challenging times,
> ***Vision***
> Declaring God's intended end in the beginning
> Is
> Spiritual Capital

REVIEW QUESTIONS

1. Considering your spiritual gifts, how will the following look three years from today?

   a. Your church:

   _____

   _____

   b. Your ministry:

   _____

   _____

   c. Your personal life:

   _____

   _____

   d. Your employment:

   _____

   _____

2. What is God's business?

   _____

   _____

Vision Is Spiritual Capital

3. What is God's vision?

   _____

   _____

*The End of the Day Meditation and Review Journal (included in this book) is designed to transfer God's vision to everyday living. Make sure to complete the End of the Day Meditation and Review Journal on a daily basis.

Take a moment and journal to God your thoughts, revelations, or reflections received from reading this Key Attribute.

Reflection: _____

_____

_____

_____

_____

KEY ATTRIBUTE 7

Faith Is Spiritual Capital

"And the Lord said, If ye had faith as a grain of mustard seed, ye might say unto this sycamine tree, Be thou plucked up by the root, and be thou planted in the sea; and it should obey you."
—Luke 17:6

Faith

Faith Is Not Believing

DURING CHALLENGING TIMES, what makes us say we are blessed when in actuality we want to give up? What is it that gives us peace of mind when we don't have the answers and we can't predict the outcome? What is it when we don't understand why we are going through what we are going through but yet we don't stop, we go through? What is it that makes us stay in God's presence even though we are tired—tired of crying, tired of hurting, and even tired of praying? Is it faith?

What is faith? In order to define what faith is, let's define what faith is not. Faith does not mean "to believe." Believing leads us to faith, but believing is not faith. Believing is validating the existence of evidence. Evidence is confirmed truth. Evidence is "the proof" that something exists. If I told you that it was snowing pink snowflakes and you had not validated that pink snowflakes exist, then you would not believe me. However, if I told you that it was hailing the size of golf balls and you had validated that hail the size of golf balls exists, then you might believe me. It was validating the existence of evidence that we were living a self-destructive, self-threatening, and sinful life that made us believe we were in need of salvation. Furthermore, it was validating the existence of evidence that in Jesus dwelt all of the "fullness of the Godhead," therefore qualifying Him as a Deliverer and a Savior (Colossians 2:9-10).

"Validating the existence of" results from the relationship between revelation and response—it is action consistent with what one confirms to be factual or true. Two examples of validating the existence of evidence can be found in Acts 16 and Luke 19. The jailer in Acts 16 validated the existence of evidence that Paul and the prisoners had fled and therefore he believed his life was over and "he drew out his sword, and would have killed himself, supposing that the prisoners had fled" (v. 27). However, when hearing Paul's voice crying, "Do thyself no harm: for we are all here" (v. 28), it was validating the existence of evidence that made the jailer tremble and fall down before Paul and Silas and ask, "What must I do to be saved?" (v. 30). In Luke 19, Zaccheus validated the existence of evidence of a sinful life as he stood and said to the Lord, "Behold, Lord, the half of my goods I give to the poor; and if I have taken any thing from any man by false accusation, I restore him fourfold" (Luke 19:8).

I remember when I validated the existence of evidence that I was living a sinful life and was in need of salvation. When I was younger, I couldn't wait to move out of my parents' house. I enjoyed living with my parents, however, there were too many restrictions. The day came when I finally moved out. Once on my own, I knew that I could not live the life I wanted and commit myself to Christian service, so I chose not to commit. My close friend saw how I was living, and she told me that Jesus was all I needed and that He would make my life complete. I remember thinking to myself that she always looked so happy and content. Sometimes she even looked as though she was glowing. I told myself that I wanted the results her life was producing. However, I wasn't ready to give up the type of life I was living. I remember telling her that I couldn't commit to a Christian lifestyle: "In the future I will, but not now—no, not now."

> *The Millionaire Christian lives by faith. When surrounded by challenging times and when life's struggles seem overwhelming, the Millionaire Christian validates the existence of God.*

One Easter Sunday this same friend called me and invited me to church. I did not want to go, but to be nice, I went. At the end of the service, the pastor invited those who wanted special prayer to approach the altar. My girlfriend nudged me and said, "Go up for special prayer." I looked at her and smiled. What she didn't hear was the sarcastic response I said quietly to myself: "Why don't you go up there for special prayer?" Before I knew it, I was walking towards the front of the church. One of the ministers approached me, grabbed my hands, and began to pray for me. While praying, I began to cry. As the tears rolled down my face, I extended my arms up above my head. I told God that I was tired of living a life controlled by my flesh. I wanted a new life. I was in need of a Deliverer. I was in need of a Savior. I validated the existence of evidence of a sinful life—a life separated from God—and I concluded that I needed Jesus.

Great Faith

To begin this discussion on faith, I would like to start with one of my favorite faith stories. The story is found in Matthew 8 and it's about the faith of the centurion. When Jesus entered Capernaum, a centurion approached Him and asked for help for his servant who was paralyzed. Jesus responded that He would go to the centurion's house and heal his servant. "The centurion answered and said, Lord, I am not worthy that thou shouldest come under my roof: but speak the word only, and my servant shall be healed, For I am a man under authority, having soldiers under me: and I say to this man, Go, and he goeth; and to another, Come, and he cometh; and to my servant, Do this, and he doeth it" (Matthew 8:8-9). When Jesus heard this He marveled, and said I have not "found so great faith" (v. 10). Such great faith!

The centurion was a commanding officer in the Roman army. As a military man, the centurion understood rank. Although he was a man in the natural, the centurion knew he was a man that was confirmed and commissioned by the military. The centurion had status and power. He knew that he stood in the place of and was the very image of a higher ruler. To disrespect and defy the centurion was to disrespect and defy the one who sent him. The centurion heard about Jesus and believed that Jesus wasn't just an ordinary man. He knew Jesus was a man with rank. He knew Jesus was commissioned and confirmed. He knew that Jesus stood in the place of and was the very image of a Higher Ruler. Jesus had status and power. To disrespect and defy Jesus was to disrespect and defy the One who sent Him. The centurion knew that Jesus was a man of authority who exercised command and control. In the military command and control is the exercise of authority used to direct and align forces and influences to the mission or desired end result. The centurion paired Jesus' command and control in the spirit realm to his command and control in the natural realm. However, it was not the pairing that demonstrated "great faith;" it was how the centurion connected to God that demonstrated "great" faith. The centurion realized that more than a mere man, more than a person in the flesh was about to enter into his home. Although he petitioned Jesus, the centurion understood that Christ, God's Anointed One, was about to enter his home. What GREAT faith! Whereas believing is validating the existence of evidence, faith is validating the existence of God.

Romans 12:3 reads: "God hath dealt to every man the measure of faith." In other words, mankind is pre-wired to connect to God. It is the will of God that all men (all mankind) be saved and to come into the knowledge of the truth (I Timothy 2:4). The provision for this will is faith. Faith works like a microchip that God placed in every individual. The microchip, called faith, is designed to automatically activate at the point of contact with

God. The one important aspect about this microchip called faith is that it requires no evidence to be activated. It's automatic at the point of contact—evidence not required!

Hebrews 11:1 says, "Now faith is the substance of things hoped for, *The evidence of things not seen.*" With faith, there is no evidence. The problem for some is the failure to activate faith—because they are looking to see what evidence exists instead of validating that God exists. Not true for the Millionaire Christian. The Millionaire Christian lives by faith. When surrounded by challenging times and when life's struggles seem overwhelming, the Millionaire Christian validates the existence of God. The Millionaire Christian tells sickness, "With His stripes I am healed" (Isaiah 53:5). The Millionaire Christian tells poverty, "God has pleasure in the prosperity of His servant" (Psalm 35:27). The Millionaire Christian tells attacks that come against their marriage, "A threefold cord is not quickly broken" (Ecclesiastes 4:12). When the enemy attacks them through their employer, the Millionaire Christian declares, "No weapon formed against me shall prosper" (Isaiah 54:17). The Millionaire Christian sees those things which are not as though they were (Romans 4:17). God is ever present and His purposeful end is happening NOW—evidence or not!

The Millionaire Christian profits from Spiritual Capital.
During challenging times,
Faith
Validating the existence of God
Is
Spiritual Capital

Faith Is Spiritual Capital

REVIEW QUESTIONS

Faith Is Not Believing

1. _____ leads you to faith.

2. Believing is _____.

3. What was your existence of evidence that lead you to Christ? (This is actually your Conversion Experience, which will be covered in more detail in Key Attribute #8.)

_____

_____

_____

_____

Example of Great Faith

1. Faith is _____ the _____ of God.

2. Some fail to activate their faith because they are looking to see what _____ exist instead of validating that _____ exist.

3. The Millionaire Christian lives by _____.

4. _____ and _____ is the exercise of _____ used to _____ and _____ forces and influences to the _____ or desired _____.

5. Using your own words, explain the difference between faith and believing.

   _____

   _____

6. The end is happening _____—evidence or not!

Take a moment and journal to God your thoughts, revelations, or reflections received from reading this Key Attribute.

Reflection: _____

_____

_____

_____

_____

KEY ATTRIBUTE 8

Knowledge Is Spiritual Capital

"By his knowledge the depths are broken up, and the clouds drop down the dew."
—Proverbs 3:20

Knowledge

THE APOSTLE PAUL knew God. According to Paul, he was "circumcised the eighth day, of the stock of Israel, of the tribe of Benjamin, an Hebrew of the Hebrews; as touching the law, a Pharisee" (Philippians 3:5). If there was one to write about the importance and significance of knowledge, I recommend no better person than the Apostle Paul.

Throughout his writings, Paul urges to grow in the knowledge of God. His prayer to the Colossians reads: "For this cause we also, since the day we heard it, do not cease to pray for you, and to desire that you might be *filled with the knowledge of his will* in all wisdom and spiritual understanding; That ye might walk worthy of the Lord unto all pleasing, being fruitful in every good work and *increasing in the knowledge of God"* (Colossians 1:9-10).

Opportunity to grow in the knowledge of God is provided through four life experiences. Each life experience ends in the accumulation of knowledge. The four life experiences are as follows:

1. Conversion
2. Cleansing
3. Conviction
4. Correction

Each life experience is:

> - Normal and typical
> - Independent and mutually exclusive
> - Comprehensive in order of occurrence
> - Successive
> - A prerequisite for the other to happen

The Millionaire Christian would never dream of confronting a challenge without the knowledge of God. The knowledge of God mirrors a life preserver—it keeps us afloat and out of harm's way—during challenging times.

The Conversion Life Experience Increases Knowledge
Knowledge is Spiritual Capital

"And it was so, that when he had turned his back to go from Samuel, God gave him another heart: and all those signs came to pass that day."
—I Samuel 10:9

Conversion

Paul was a man with a mission. He was determined to persecute Christians. What he did not know was that God had other plans for him. Paul was no stranger to Christianity as he stood front and center when Stephen was stoned to death (Acts 7). What a landmark speech and a great testimony of the gospel Stephen gave as he answered charges of blasphemy. I personally believe that his speech paved the way to Paul's conversion. If not, it was definitely a turning point in Paul's life, as in Acts 22:20 Paul recounted the death of Stephen. Nonetheless, Paul guarded the clothes of those who stoned Stephen and consented to his death.

What we must remember is that the book of Acts was written by Luke. Therefore, Luke is writing about Paul's conversion experience and not Paul himself. Paul commented on his own conversion in Galatians 1:15-17. Nonetheless, Luke provides more details of this life turning experience. According to Luke, Paul (then Saul) was traveling with letters written to the synagogues in Damascus granting him permission to imprison Christians (be it man or woman). As Saul came near Damascus, a light came from heaven and he fell to the ground. A voice spoke: "Saul, Saul, why persecutest thou me?" Saul responded,

"Who art thou, Lord?" The answer: "I am Jesus, whom thou persecutest" (Acts 9:4-5). According to Luke, the men traveling with Saul heard the voice but saw no man. When Saul got up, he was blind. After the encounter, (according to Paul, as he wrote in Galatians 1), he went to Arabia.

Conversion is a pinnacle experience. It begins when we accept the reality that we need God. We realize that what we are facing is bigger than ourselves and it will take a greater power to deliver us and to make the mess go away. Therefore, we make a conscious decision to believe the gospel of Jesus Christ. For the first time we see the vast difference between living a life controlled by sin and a life controlled by the Spirit. The conversion experience tells our salvation story. It is our message to the world confirming that there is a God and that Jesus is real. It's our personal legacy to our family, friends, and even to our enemies. The conversion encounter is usually our first personal encounter with Christ. Can you recall your conversion experience? What is your salvation story? If you have no salvation story to tell, then make today your conversion day. Pray this prayer:

> "God, I know that I have willingly made decisions that went against your divine standards as to how I should live this life that you graciously gave to me. I ask you to forgive me. I confess with my mouth that Jesus is Lord and I believe in my heart that Jesus Christ is the Son of God, the Word made flesh. I believe that Jesus came to the earth; He lived, died, He was raised from the dead, and He will come again. I repent and turn away from sin, from those thoughts, emotions, feelings, actions, and behaviors that were against your divine standards, and I present my body, a living sacrifice, holy and

acceptable unto you. I make you, Jesus, Lord and Savior over my life. Holy Spirit, I welcome you into this temple to dwell, to reign, to empower, to lead, and to guide me. God, I believe that you will be with me and I with you for eternity and that I am saved from sin, self, the grave, and death. In Jesus Christ's name I pray. Amen."

_____   _____
Your Signature   Date

If you prayed this prayer, then I encourage you to contact your pastor and share your conversion experience.

The Cleansing Life Experience Increases Knowledge Knowledge is Spiritual Capital

"Create in me a clean heart, O God; and renew a right spirit within me."
—Psalm 51:10

Cleansing

The second life experience that increases the knowledge of God is the Cleansing Life Experience. When we surrender our life to Jesus Christ, we place at His feet our brokenness, scars, and wounds. Some of us have been abused, misused, and degraded. Some came to Jesus Christ needing surgery, some stitching, and some bandaging. I remember when I turned my life over to Jesus. The next day, although I looked the same, I felt different. I couldn't really explain it, but I knew that something happened to me at that church the night before. I couldn't feel it. I couldn't see it. Nor could I taste it. But deep down inside of me, I knew that I was changed. I knew that the change was nothing I concocted. I knew that God changed me. I wanted to know more about this change. I wanted to know more about God. So I began reading the Bible. Then another strange thing happened to me. The more I read, the more revelations I received. The more revelations I received, the more I understood. The more I understood, the more my desires changed. As my knowledge of God increased, those sinful and un-God-like desires decreased. A cleansing process began in me.

Everyone has a way. The Bible says, "There is a way that seemeth right unto a man, but the end thereof are the ways of death" (Proverbs 16:25). "Way" is a specific habitual manner of behaving or doing that produces a specific order of how things are to happen. When we cling to our specific, habitual manner of behaving or doing, we determine the order of how things are suppose to happen. Clinging to our way ends in death, a spiritual separation from God. We must make habit God's way of behaving and doing so that God's order will happen.

> *The Millionaire Christian refuses to accept the bondage mentality. The bondage mentality leads to the belief that change is impossible. The Millionaire Christian believes that change is possible—with God all things are possible (Mark 10:27).*

Cleansing is a life experience where God implants His compass; He sets His direction and programs His way for our lives. During the Cleansing Life Experience, our soul, mind, and spirit lay exposed before God while He removes every thought, plan, and emotion that signals a path contrary to His way or direction. Cleansing is what God had to do to the Israelites after they were released from Egypt. The Israelites had been slaves to the Egyptians for many generations. The time of deliverance came and God used Moses to lead the Israelites to the "Promised Land." Scripture reads: "When Pharaoh had let the people go, that God led them not through the way of the land of the Philistines, although that was near; for God said, lest peradventure the people repent when they see war, and they return to Egypt" (Exodus 13:17).

The Israelites had a bondage mentality. Their way of acting, thinking, and believing was under the control of the Egyptians and not under God's control. They did not know who they were. More importantly, they did not know whose they were. Remember the negative report that came before Moses after the spies had explored the land of Canaan? Numbers 13 records that the spies returned from spying the land and said (paraphrased), "Oh yeah, Moses, we explored the land that you said God will give us and sure, it flows with milk and honey. Look at this big piece of fruit we took from the land. But what God failed to tell you was that the people who live there are strong and very large and the cities are walled. By the way, Moses, we saw the sons of Anak there. You know the sons of Anak, they are great and mighty. Hello? Giants! We were in our own sights as grasshoppers, and so we were in their sight."

The Israelites saw themselves as grasshoppers when compared to the enemy. This was the result of that bondage mentality. Scared, always scared. Uncertain about what you can do. Always questioning the results. "What if this happens?" You are always the victim, never the victor. You don't trust your own opinion. You compulsively and excessively seek the advice of others. You feel helpless—looking for the Controller to do what you can so easily do for yourself. You're angry, just angry. You are not only angry because of your bondage lifestyle, you are angry because you have become comfortable with your bondage lifestyle. It's that bondage mentality.

I have a little Shih Tzu (mixed with terrier) named Alex. Alex is a small dog. I say sometimes jokingly that he's no bigger than an ant. However, when confronted by a Great Dane that lives in our neighborhood, Alex barks and jumps around like he's three times bigger than the Great Dane. I mean, he's pulling me and ferociously growling like he can whip the color off that dog. Alex knows that the Great Dane is another dog, but what Alex doesn't factor in is that the other dog is about ten times bigger than he is. In Alex's mind, he's bigger than that Great Dane. Alex has a "more than a conqueror" mentality. That's the same mentality we operate in when under God's control. When confronted with a challenge or a difficult situation, we ferociously attack. In our minds we are bigger than that challenge or difficult situation. In our mind we are more than conquerors (Romans 8:37).

Our response also mimics that of Caleb and Joshua. When confronted with the negative report, Caleb said, "Let us go up at once, and possess it; for we are well able to overcome it" (Numbers 13:30). Joshua and Caleb said, "They are bread for us: their defense is departed from them, and the Lord is with us: fear them not" (Numbers 14:9).

When we decide in our minds that the issue we are confronting is a challenge, it is not a challenge anymore—now it has become our way of living, our reality. When we decide that we are "more than conquerors," the perception of challenge is silenced and God's reality is revealed.

Three Realities Resulting from the Cleansing Life Experience:

1. **God is in Control**—We realize that we do not and can not control the outcome. God controls the outcome. We are not responsible for the outcome. God is responsible for the outcome.
2. **Increased Intimacy**—Have you ever had a particular life experience to keep repeating itself? God will allow the same life experience or predicament to repeat over and over again. Why? Intimacy with God increases through repeated experiences. Our prayers become longer and our love for God grows stronger. Repeated life experiences engrave God's pathways and help us to realize the underlying motive provoking our behavioral and emotional responses. Repeated life experiences prompt us to ponder our actions and measure our choices through and against the word of God.
3. **No More Straddling the Fence**—When we "straddle the fence" our life resembles a chameleon—our lifestyle changes with our surrounding. When surrounded by Christians, we respond sinlessly. When surrounded by the world, we respond sinfully. Straddling the fence exposes our spiritual condition. As we straddle the fence,

we come to realize that we must choose between pleasing God and pleasing the world.

The Millionaire Christian refuses to accept the bondage mentality. The bondage mentality leads to the belief that change is impossible. The Millionaire Christian believes that change is possible—with God all things are possible (Mark 10:27).

The Cleansing Life Experience is a funnel that leads to increased knowledge of God and makes evident God's way. Our knowledge of God increases when we choose His way.

The Conviction Life Experience Increases Knowledge
Knowledge is Spiritual Capital

"But we had the sentence of death in ourselves, that we should not trust in ourselves, but in God which raiseth the dead: Who delivered us from so great a death, and doth deliver: in whom we trust that he will deliver us..."
—2 Corinthians 1:9-10

Conviction

The third life experience that increases knowledge is the Conviction Life Experience. As a babe in Christ, I was born with a hunger and thirst to know God. I took off running. I was reading the Bible multiple times a day and witnessing nearly every time I opened my mouth. I knew that I had been changed and I was not afraid to share it. In the mid 1980's, I worked at a group home for girls on the north side of Chicago. I was just born into Christ and I thought my mission was to allow God to use me to change these young girls' lives. Little did I know that it was my life that was about to be changed. I worked a sixteen hour shift, 3:00 P.M. to 7:00 A.M. three days a week. The routine for starting a shift was to first do what we called an "Overlap" (briefing) with the staff leaving for the day. The Overlap was held in the kitchen as the kitchen was the quasi staff office. After the Overlap, the next duty was to read the daily log which documented in detail the girls' behavior and any incidents that happened that day. Now when I arrived to work, the girls were just arriving home from school. I remember I would always start my shift in the kitchen with the daily log and a cigarette. It never seemed to fail that every time I was smoking, one particular girl would always walk into the kitchen. Sometimes when she entered, I would have a cigarette in one hand and the Bible in the other hand. One day when she walked into the kitchen, I began witnessing of God's goodness and power. I was trying to minister a change in her life when she said to me, "If God is so good and so powerful then how come you are hooked on cigarettes?" Here I was telling this young lady that God was so good and that He was all she ever needed and she snapped back with, "Then why is smoking controlling you?" For the first time I asked myself, *Is smoking controlling me?* More importantly I thought, *Do I look like Jesus? She did not see Jesus in me.*

> *The Millionaire Christian treasures understanding and heeds conviction. The Millionaire Christian refuses to believe a lie and therefore uses conviction to amplify the leading of the Holy Spirit and to regain position in the will of God.*

By the time this happened to me, I had much of God's word in me. I knew Him. The question then became, "Will I lean to my knowledge of God and let my understanding of who God is define me?" Conviction hit home. Conviction is the presence of spiritual, emotional, and/or mental conflict resulting from inconsistency between what one understands to be true about God and the urge to act opposite of that understanding. For me, smoking was just the symptom. The real truth of the matter was that the addiction to smoke had a control, a powerful influence over my life. The addiction shaped and dictated my actions. I was supposed to be Holy Spirit-filled and Holy Spirit-led. However, in this situation, the Holy Spirit was not leading me and the Holy Spirit was not controlling me.

Proverbs 4:7 says in all your getting, "get understanding." Understanding breeds conviction. Conviction can only emerge in the presence of understanding. No understanding, no conviction. Luke 22 records one of the most touching conviction stories in the Bible. The chapter unfolds Jesus' betrayal. Judas betrayed Jesus, and Jesus was arrested and taken to the house of the high priest. Peter followed and sat among others near a fire in the middle of the courtyard. Now Jesus had already told Peter that before the cock crowed, Peter would three times deny that he knew Jesus. Well, here is Peter warming himself by the fire when a servant girl saw him seated there in the firelight. She looked closely at him and recalled that Peter was with Jesus (Luke 22:56). Peter denied it. A little later someone else saw him and alleged that Peter was a follower of Jesus (Luke 22:58). Peter denied it. About an hour later another alleged again that Peter was a follower, as he was a Galilean (Luke 22:59). Peter denied it. "And the Lord turned, and looked upon Peter. And

Peter remembered the word of the Lord, how he had said unto him Before the cock crow, thou shalt deny me thrice. And Peter went out, and wept bitterly" (Luke 22:61-62).

    Peter was hurt because Peter understood. It wasn't so much that Peter understood that Jesus was right—he would deny Him three times. Moreover, Peter understood that he himself was wrong. Peter was overly confident in himself. When Jesus told Peter that he would deny Him three times, Peter responded, "Lord I am ready to go with thee, both into prison, and to death" (Luke 22:33). Peter was actually saying, "Jesus, I got your back." Have you ever been in a situation where someone told you, "I got your back?" However, when the time of performance came, it was just the opposite—they stabbed you in the back. Was Peter not sincere? Peter was every bit sincere. Nonetheless he denied acknowledging his weakness in spite of Jesus just telling him, "Simon, Simon, behold, Satan hath desired to have you, that he may sift you as wheat; But I have prayed for thee, that thy faith fail not: and when thou art converted, strengthen thy brethren" (Luke 22:31-32). In other words, Jesus said to Peter, "Hey Peter, you call yourself a follower. Satan doesn't seem to think so. Satan thinks if he causes some turbulence in your life—put you in a 'fight or flight' situation, that your true colors will come out and show you're no follower after all." Peter did not say, "Pray for me now" or "Be my strength" or "Help me, Jesus." No, instead Peter responded, "I got this." However, when the truth was revealed, Peter was able to discern between what he thought was true and what reality proved to be true. Peter understood and felt convicted.

Discernment precedes understanding. Discernment is the ability to detect the spiritual from the natural. When we detect the spiritual from the natural, we are better equipped to hear from God via filling in the gaps, sorting the information, and grouping into categories. Discernment helps us to distinguish and dissect if something is of God or not. We gain a spiritual understanding thereby enabling us to make informed and educated decisions that will result in a balanced life—a life inspired by God. During challenging times, living a balanced life is crucial. Proverbs 11:1 reads: "A false balance is abomination to the Lord: but a just weight is his delight." A false balance represents a lie. Failure to get an understanding and failure to discern represents a false balance—a life not inspired by God. To represent a false balance is to live a lie, and to live a lie is disgusting to God. Peter's response to Jesus was not inspired by God. Therefore, Peter lived a lie. Peter did not have a clue as to the spiritual revolution that the death of Jesus was about to stir. Yet he projected that he did. His ignorance of the matter led to his conviction.

In closing, conviction is similar to a burglar alarm. The purpose of a burglar alarm is to make the intruder aware that the owner has set up a special communication system and if the intruder's language does not match the language programmed by the owner, then a warning signal will sound. The warning signal tells the owner that a thief is on the premises. Such is true of conviction. Conviction signals a warning to the Christian that communication with God (via the Holy Spirit) has been broken and a thief is on the premises. Should the Christian fail to put up a defense and restore communication, then the thief will steal, maybe even kill, but definitely will destroy and separate the Christian from the will of God.

The Millionaire Christian treasures understanding and heeds conviction. The Millionaire Christian refuses to believe a lie and therefore uses conviction to amplify the leading of the Holy Spirit and to regain position in the will of God.

The Correction Life Experience Increases Knowledge Knowledge is Spiritual Capital

> "Search me, O God, and know my heart: try me and know my thoughts. And see if there be any wicked way in me, and lead me in the way everlasting."
> —Psalm 139:23-24

Correction

It is within the Correction Life Experience that we see the greatest demonstration of God's patience towards us. Here we face our consequences and we acknowledge our sins. Our prayers are carefully analyzed as we flush our spirit and soul of every selfish motive and ambition. Because past life experiences vary from Christian to Christian, God's correction also varies. However, one common encounter found within this life experience is the struggle with delayed answers to prayers. Two common ways answers to prayers are delayed are through praying amiss and our failure to delight in the Lord.

Praying Amiss

James 4:3 reads: "Ye ask, and receive not, because ye ask amiss that ye may consume it upon your lusts." "Amiss" is *kakos* in the Greek, and it means "wrongly." Therefore, praying amiss is praying wrongly—praying with wrong motives. A motive is that bottom line urge that pulls, tugs, and impels us to pray. I remember when I prayed amiss for a husband. What was my motive? Plain and simple, I wanted to be married. It wasn't until I was reading I Samuel 8 that I received the revelation that my motives for a husband were wrong and selfish. Samuel was old, so he appointed his sons as judges over Israel. The problem with this was that Samuel's sons did not walk in the way of God as Samuel walked. So Israel asked for a king. Israel told Samuel that they wanted to be like the other nations that had a king, and they wanted a king, too. This displeased Samuel, and Samuel prayed to the Lord. "And the Lord said unto Samuel, hearken unto the voice of the people in all that they say unto thee: for they have not rejected thee, but they have rejected me, that I should not reign over them" (I Samuel 8:7). After reading, I shook my head in disappointment. "The nerve of them to ask for a king," I said. God responded to me, "You're asking for a king." I responded, "What are you talking about?" God said, "You're praying for a husband." I responded, "And?" God said to me, "And I am your Husband. When you pray for a husband, you are rejecting me as your Husband." (*See note)

My prayer request for a husband was amiss just like the Israelites' request for a king. We both had wrong motives. Our bottom line urge that impelled us to pray was according to our desires and not God's desires. The Israelites desired a king to go before them and to fight their battles (I Samuel 8:19-20). Where was a king when the Israelites were trapped between Pharaoh's army and the Red Sea (Exodus 14:13-31)? God was their King! Where was a king when the Amalekites attacked and as long as Moses' hands were uplifted, the Israelites won, but when his arms were lowered they lost and Aaron and Hur held up Moses' hand, one on one side, one on the other, and the Amalekites were defeated (Exodus 17:8-16)? God was their King! Where was a king when the Israelites marched around the wall of Jericho and the "wall fell down flat" (Joshua 6)? There was no king. God was their King!

Here I was, always the bridesmaid and never the bride. It seemed as though all of my friends were getting married. I just desired what my friends had. What was wrong with that? Everything was wrong with that! God said to me, "When all four of your tires were badly worn and you needed a new set, you left the shop with four new tires on your car. Where was your husband? I was your Husband! When your landlord had to sell the house you were renting and you had nowhere to go, financing was arranged and you were able to buy the house from her—taking you from a tenant to a homeowner. Where was your husband? I was your Husband! When you ended a day's work feeling overwhelmed and you were crying, hugging your pillow tight, wishing for morning, you woke up the next morning with hope and encouragement to start a brand new day. Where was your husband? I was your Husband!" God was hurt. I prayed amiss.

Delight In the Lord

Psalm 37:4 reads: "Delight thyself also in the Lord; and he shall give thee the desires of thine heart." Now I have heard it said over and over that this scripture means that whatever you desire, God will give it to you. I beg to differ. So often the first part of the scripture is overlooked and we immediately jump to the second part as if the scripture reads: "God will give you the desires of your heart." What I believe this scripture is saying is that if you make God the only force in your life that is capable of shaping you, directing you, and influencing you, then God will *share* His desires with you. Therefore, the desires you have will come from God, will be His desires and not your own. God will place His desires in your heart.

We delight in the Lord—make God the only force that is capable of shaping, directing and influencing us—when we speak the same language as God and when we wait on God.

Speak the same language

In order to speak the same language as God, we must learn His language. God's language is contained within the Bible—it is His word. Delighting ourselves in God requires us to learn scripture to the point that we connect and trace our actions and reactions to God's word. The scriptures must become our primary language to the point where just the knowledge of scripture evokes a reflexive Christ-like response to every situation.

Wait on God

When the Israelites sought a king, God chose Saul to be king. The prophet Samuel took a flask of oil and poured it on Saul's head and Saul was officially anointed king over God's people. Afterwards, Samuel sent Saul on his way and prophetically told Saul all that would happen to him on his journey. Samuel said to Saul, "And thou shalt go down before me to Gilgal; and, behold, I will come down unto thee, to offer burnt offerings, and to sacrifice sacrifices of peace offerings: seven days shalt thou tarry, till I come to thee, and show thee what thou shalt do" (I Samuel 10:8). Samuel told Saul to wait seven days.

"Wait" means to look with eager expectation. The best way I can describe how we are to wait is remembering back to when I was a child. As a child, I played many games, but the game which I can use to best describe how Saul was suppose to wait and how we are suppose to wait is Freeze Tag. As I recall, someone has the "Freeze Touch." If this person touches you, you automatically become "frozen." You must stay in a frozen position until someone unfreezes you. While you are waiting, it is with eager expectation that someone would run by you, touch you, and unfreeze you.

Samuel's command to wait was the "Freeze Touch." Saul was to act frozen and in eager expectation of Samuel's return. However, with heavy artillery and troops that number like the sand on the seashore, the Philistines assembled to fight Israel. The Israelites saw that the situation was critical and they hid in caves, holes, rocks, tombs, and pits. While waiting the seven days for Samuel, Saul got impatient—"And he tarried seven days, according to the set time that Samuel had appointed: but Samuel came not to Gilgal; and the people were scattered from him. And Saul said, Bring hither a burnt offering

> *The Correction Life Experience produces character and differentiates the Me Christian from the Millionaire Christian. Unanswered prayers become answered prayers because the Millionaire Christian has made God the only force that is capable of shaping, directing, and influencing them.*

to me, and peace offerings. And he offered burnt offering" (I Samuel 13:8-9). Saul's offering of the burnt offering violated the office of the priest. It was not Saul's place or position to offer an offering before God. But Saul gave in to impatience.

Impatience results from the perception and acceptance of the unexpected, unavoidable, and uncontrollable as impending or real. In essence, we judge the experience as real and critical and therefore give up on God and refuse to wait for God to answer. The mode of thinking then becomes, "If you want something done right, you better do it yourself." Impatience makes us believe, "This is getting out of control and something needs to be done," and "If this doesn't stop, then something bad is going to happen. I must do something!" God is removed from the driver's seat and we begin to dictate to God how things will happen. The end result is that God's will is abandoned and we settle for second best.

A Millionaire Christian doesn't settle for second best. They wait for God's best. Did you settle for second best? Is the life you are now living a result of being impatient? Did you make a foolish decision and judge a life experience as critical and real? If so, it is not too late to return to your first Love. Repent for not waiting. Ask God for forgiveness and commit yourself to waiting on God.

In conclusion, knowledge is the fuel that fans the fire of spiritual growth. The Correction Life Experience produces character and differentiates the *Me* Christian from the Millionaire Christian. Unanswered prayers become answered prayers because the Millionaire Christian has made God the only force that is capable of shaping, directing, and influencing them.

Knowledge Is Spiritual Capital

The Millionaire Christian profits from Spiritual Capital.
During challenging times,
Knowledge
Receiving Jesus Christ as the atonement for sin, pursing His way, heeding His truth, and waiting for His answers
Is
Spiritual Capital

*This is what God ministered to me in my particular situation. Unless God has spoken otherwise, do not personalize this statement.

Review Questions

Knowledge

1. The four life experiences where we accumulate knowledge are:

   _____, _____,

   _____, _____.

Conversion Life Experience

1. Conversion is a _____ experience.

2. We accept the _____ that we need God.

3. The conversion experience tells our _____ story.

4. The conversion experience is our _____ legacy to our family, friends, and even to our enemies.

5. Tell your salvation story. Write your conversion experience (reference your answer for #3 on Faith Key Attribute).

   _____

   _____

   _____

   _____

Cleansing Life Experience

1. Explain the statement "Everyone has a way."

   _____

   _____

2. Clinging to our way ends in _____, a spiritual _____ from God.

3. We must make _____ God's way of behaving and doing so that God's _____ will happen.

4. During the Cleansing Life Experience, our _____ and _____ lay exposed before God while He removes every _____, _____, and _____ that sings a path contrary to His _____ or _____.

5. Briefly share your Cleansing Life Experience.

   _____

   _____

   _____

6. What is your definition of the "bondage mentality"?

   _____

   _____

7. Write about a situation that keeps repeating in your life? What do you think God is trying to uncover or reveal?

   _____

   _____

   _____

8. When we judge our challenge as a _____, it is not a _____ anymore—now it has become our _____, our _____.

9. Which of the three realities have you personally experienced?

   _____

   _____

Conviction Life Experience

1. Do you look like Jesus? If no, then why not?

   _____

   _____

2. Proverbs 4:7 reads: "In all of your _____ understanding.

3. _____ breeds conviction.

4. Discernment precedes _____.

5. Write about a time in our life when you discerned between the truth and a lie.

   _____

   _____

6. Write about what conviction means to you.

   _____

   _____

7. A _____ balance represents _____.

8. Was there ever a time that you lived a lie—when your life was not inspired by God? If yes, explain. If no, then why not?

   _____

   _____

Correction Life Experience

1. It is within the Correction Life Experience that we see the greatest demonstration of God's _____.

2. Two common ways prayers are delayed are through _____ and failure to _____ ourselves in the _____.

3. What is the definition of "praying amiss"?

   _____

4. Write about a time when you prayed amiss.

   _____

   _____

5. We delight ourselves in the Lord when we _____ and we _____.

6. Wait means to look with _____ expectations.

7. Impatience results from the _____ and _____ of the _____, _____, _____ as pending or real.

8. Write about a time when you settled for second best.

   _____

   _____

Take a moment and journal to God your thoughts, revelations, or reflections received from reading this Key Attribute.

Reflection: _____

_____

_____

_____

_____

KEY ATTRIBUTE 9

Wisdom Is Spiritual Capital

"But wisdom is justified of all of her children."
—Luke 7:35

Wisdom

THE BIBLE REFERS to King Solomon as the wisest person of all times. Solomon was the second child born to David and Bathsheba (their first died as a child—2 Samuel 12:18). Solomon was appointed next in line to become king (I Chronicles 22:9-10). However, his half brother Adonijah decided to beat him to the throne and announced himself king of Israel instead of Solomon. The news was brought to David's attention and David anointed and established Solomon as king in his stead.

When Solomon's throne was established, "the Lord appeared to Solomon in a dream by night: and God said, Ask what I shall give thee" (I Kings 3:5). Solomon asked for an understanding heart. However, read closely as to what God actually gave him—"Behold, I have done according to thy words: lo, I have given thee a wise and an understanding heart: so that there was none like thee before thee, neither shall any arise like unto thee" (I Kings 3:12). Solomon asked for understanding and God gave him wisdom.

Three Working Definitions and Images of Wisdom

The Bible offers many definitions and comparisons of wisdom, for example: "Wisdom is justified of her children" (Matthew 11:19). Also, "For wisdom is better than rubies; and all the things that may be desired are not compared to it" (Proverbs 8:11). In order to better understand what wisdom is, the following discussion will illustrate how wisdom operates.

I. Wisdom Deficiency Syndrome

Wisdom is an authorization to impart, apply, and reproduce God's power and authority. James 1:5 reads: "If any of you lack wisdom, let him ask of God, that giveth to all men liberally, and upbraideth not; and it shall be given him." This scripture prescribes the antidote when experiencing what I will refer to as "Wisdom Deficiency Syndrome." For the purpose of this attribute, Wisdom Deficiency Syndrome is the inability to impart, apply, and reproduce God's power and authority. Symptoms of Wisdom Deficiency Syndrome include (but are not limited to) responding powerlessly or seeking permission to exercise power and authority.

In Luke 4, Jesus was in Capernaum teaching on the Sabbath. And in the synagogue, there was a man that had an "unclean devil" and he cried out with a loud voice. Jesus rebuked the devil and commanded the devil to come out of the man. "And they were all amazed, and spake among themselves, saying, What a word is this! For with authority and power he commandeth unclean spirits, and they come out" (Luke 4:36). Jesus exercised *authority* and *power*. He didn't whine or beg. Nor did Jesus seek permission. He commanded! Jesus engaged wisdom. He imparted, applied, and reproduced God's authority and power.

> *When facing challenging times, we only see what's presented before us. The good news is that wisdom keeps us in the presence of God and aligns our decisions to His word. And if there's ever a time when we don't know what to do, all we have to do is ask.*

Authority is the ability to enforce. Power is the ability to produce results. One could have the ability to enforce without the ability to produce results, and vice versa, the ability to produce results but no ability to enforce. For example, a church pastor has the ability to enforce. However the ability to produce results could be tainted by controlling personalities—overbearing, pushy "membership cliques" in the church. Therefore, although the pastor can enforce, there is no power to produce results—thus giving rise to Wisdom Deficiency Syndrome.

When experiencing Wisdom Deficiency Syndrome, we become easily frustrated. Our thinking becomes contaminated and we see ourselves losing instead of winning. In a desperate moment, we turn to God and we pray for wisdom. However, confusion takes a common lead, and when petitioning God for wisdom, our prayers often include the request for knowledge and understanding. In order to properly cure Wisdom Deficiency Syndrome and to prevent a major and/or minor relapse, we must know the difference between wisdom, knowledge, and understanding.

- Understanding leads to habits—habits **equip** us to be effective and efficient
- Knowledge leads to competence—competence **qualifies** us to be effective and efficient
- Wisdom leads to achievement—achievement **validates** us to be effective and efficient

The Cure for Wisdom Deficiency Syndrome

When our spirit becomes diseased with Wisdom Deficiency Syndrome, the cure according to James 1:5 is to "ask of God." Therefore, when we lack the ability to impart, apply, and reproduce God's authority and power, we should not seek instruction from the world as to the best and proper way to exercise authority and power; we should seek instruction from God as to the best and proper way to exercise authority and power. We ask God.

II. Deadbolt Lock

Wisdom simulates a deadbolt lock. When I moved out of my parents' home and to my own apartment, many people told me to invest in a deadbolt lock. They said that these types of locks are good because when locking the door, the bolt is extended into the doorframe, thereby preventing easy access.

The doorframe would have to be damaged or the door physically removed in order to gain entry. Also, it is difficult to maneuver the bolt without a key. A burglar could not use some type of tool to push back the bolt and unlock the door. Wisdom is our deadbolt lock. During challenging times, our circumstances can cause us to question God's word—*did God really say*? Like a thief, challenging times causes us to doubt God and rob us from receiving answered prayers. Wisdom keeps us bolted to God. Although the thief can knock (via temptation) he cannot enter unless he destroys our faith and separates us from God. Wisdom prevents the thief from entering and from trespassing onto God's property. Wisdom extends through our circumstance, affixes us to God's word, and directs God's presence into every challenging situation.

III. Order of Protection

Wisdom functions like an order of protection. Years ago I worked as a project administrator for a Domestic Violence Agency. My office was located in the courthouse, where I assisted victims of domestic violence with filing for an order of protection. It saddened me to witness these victims suffering hurt at the hands of another. Yet my job was to help them end a dangerous and potentially fatal situation. An order of protection is a court order designed to protect the victim and to stop the abuse. The victim petitions the court for an order of protection and a judge grants the order. The victim leaves the courthouse with papers signed by a judge with legal restrictions intended for the abuser based on the victim's request. The order itself is pieces of paper. The power of the order surfaces when the victim enforces the order contingent on the abuser's violation. If the victim chooses not to enforce the order, the order cannot fulfill its purpose. An order of protection must be enforced.

Just like the order of protection, wisdom must be enforced. We can accept wisdom from God and choose to remain spiritually powerless and intimidated, just like the victim of abuse can accept an order of protection from the judge and choose to remain in danger. When a victim fails to enforce an order of protection, they give authority and power to the abuser and the abuser controls the victim. The same applies with wisdom. When wisdom doesn't empower us through challenging times, we give authority and power to our intelligence, and our intellect controls us during challenging times. The order of protection is the victim's instrument to legally enforce the judge's restrictions. Wisdom is our instrument to legally impart, apply, and reproduce God's power and authority.

When facing challenging times, we only see what's presented before us. The good news is that wisdom keeps us in the presence of God and aligns our decisions to His word. And if there's ever a time when we don't know what to do, all we have to do is ask.

> The Millionaire Christian profits from Spiritual Capital.
> During challenging times,
> ***Wisdom***
> Imparting, applying, and reproducing God's authority
> Is
> Spiritual Capital

Wisdom Is Spiritual Capital

Review Questions

1. Wisdom is an authorization to _____, _____, and _____ God's power and authority.

2. According to James 1:5, if we lack wisdom we should _____ of God.

3. Wisdom Deficiency Syndrome occurs when we respond _____ or _____ permission to exercise authority.

4. What is Wisdom Deficiency Syndrome?

   _____

   _____

   _____

5. Authority is the favor to _____.

6. Power is the favor to _____ _____.

7. Write about a time when you had authority but had no power.

   _____

   _____

   _____

8. Match the following:

   Understanding   Qualifies

   Wisdom   Validates

   Knowledge   Equips

9. Recall a time when you failed to use wisdom. What were the consequences?

   _____

   _____

   _____

10. Wisdom simulates a _____ lock.

11. Wisdom keeps us _____ to God.

12. Wisdom prevents the thief from _____ and _____ on to God's property.

13. Wisdom _____ through our circumstance, _____ us to God's word, and _____ God's presence into every challenging situation.

14. Wisdom functions like an _____ of _____.

15. Wisdom must be _____.

16. We can accept wisdom from God and _____ to remain spiritually _____ and _____.

17. When wisdom fails to _____ us through challenging times, we give _____ and _____ to our _____, and _____ assumes control over challenging times.

Take a moment and journal to God your thoughts, revelations, or reflections received from reading this Key Attribute.

Reflection: _____
_____
_____
_____
_____

KEY ATTRIBUTE 10

Sovereignty Is Spiritual Capital

"In whom we have obtained an inheritance, being predestinated according to the purpose of him who worketh all things after the counsel of his own will..."
—Ephesians 1:11

Sovereignty

THE PREVIOUS NINE attributes are considered personal attributes. Personal attributes are possessed within the person. This last attribute, sovereignty, belongs to God—it is one that God possesses. It is pertinent that we adopt and apply this attribute during challenging times.

God is sovereign! He is the Supreme and Ultimate Authority. God needs not consult with anyone or anything. He is the Creator, the originator, and the Dictator. God is unlimited. God is so unlimited that when Moses asked Him, "Behold, when I come unto the children of Israel, and shall say unto them, The

God of your fathers hast sent me unto you; and they shall say to me, What is his name? what shall I say unto them?" (Exodus 3:13). God answered, "I AM THAT I AM" (Exodus 3:14). In short, God was telling Moses, I AM everything you can think of and everything you cannot think of and when you think you know who I AM, I AM more than that.

God is so awesome that He made a name for Himself that carries power and authority, "that at the name of Jesus every knee should bow, of things in heaven, and things in earth, and things under the earth; And that every tongue should confess that Jesus Christ is Lord, to the glory of God the Father" (Philippians 2:10). We cannot survive challenging times without Jesus. Jesus is the way, the truth, and the light (John 14:6). When challenging times take us to the point where we feel as though everything is out of control and we are at the brink of losing our mind, Jesus is our Peace (John 14:27). When life pressures and demands feel as though they are literally suffocating us and we have no strength to retaliate, Jesus

Challenging times can make us feel as though we are caught in a storm. Life's pressures resemble heavy, violent winds. We are tossed to and fro. Sometimes our only recourse is to close our eyes and to pray for morning to come. We have weighed all of our options. We have considered all alternatives. In a desperate moment, we stop and realize that God is sovereign, and the heavy wind ceases to roar.

is our Deliverer (2 Timothy 4:16-18). When sin condemns us and makes us wish that we were dead, Jesus is our Advocate (I John 2:1). When family and friends alienate us and treat us as if we don't exist, Jesus is our Friend (John 15:15). During challenging times, Jesus is our help—He is our Bridge to victory!

During challenging times, we must recall God's victories. We must tap into the knowledge that Moses demonstrated when God was angry with the Israelites and wanted to annihilate them. Spies were sent to explore Canaan. After hearing the report from the spies, the people rebelled against God, saying, "And wherefore hath the Lord brought us unto this land, to fall by the sword, that our wives and our children should be prey? Were it not better for us to return into Egypt? And they said one to another, Let us make a captain, and let us return into Egypt" (Numbers 14:3-4). God responded that he would smite them with pestilence and dispose of them and use Moses to make a greater and mightier nation.

> "And Moses said unto the Lord, Then the Egyptians shall hear it, (for thou broughtest up this people in thy might from among them;) And they will tell it to the inhabitants of this land: for they have heard that thou Lord art among this people, that thou Lord art seen face to face, and that thy cloud standeth over them, and that thou goest before them by day time in a pillar of a cloud, and in a pillar of fire by night. Now if thou shalt kill all this people as one man, then the nations which have heard the fame of thee will speak, saying, Because the Lord was not able to bring this people into the land which he sware unto them, therefore he hath slain them in the wilderness. And now, I beseech

thee, let the power of my Lord be great, according as thou hast spoken, saying, The Lord is longsuffering, and of great mercy, forgiving iniquity and transgression, and by no means clearing the guilty, visiting the iniquity of the fathers upon the children unto the third and fourth generation. Pardon, I beseech thee, the iniquity of this people according unto the greatness of thy mercy, and thou hast forgiven this people, from Egypt even until now."

—Numbers 14:13-19

Moses understood that God made a name for Himself. God established a reputation, a track record as being the Almighty God, the Powerful God, the Merciful God, the Loving God, and the Great God! In all agreement, the people were disobedient. They disrespected God and rebelled. By all right God could have wiped them from the face of the earth. However, Moses understood that actions speak louder than words and although the people's actions deserved such consequences, Moses appealed to God, but not on behalf of the people. Moses appealed to God for His name's sake.

Jeremiah said it best: "O Lord, though our iniquities testify against us, do thou it for thou name's sake; for our backslidings are many; we have sinned against thee" (Jeremiah 14:7). When David's enemies came against him and they laid nets, in secret, for him, David appealed to God and said, "For Thou art my rock and my fortress; for Thy name's sake Thou wilt lead me and guide me" (Psalm 31:3). When referring to Israel as stubborn and hardheaded, God declared, "For my name's sake will I defer my anger, and for my praise will I refrain for thee, that I cut thee not off" (Isaiah 48:9).

Sovereignty Is Spiritual Capital

When we petition God on behalf of His name's sake, we are surrendering to His purpose. We are communicating to God our willingness and our decision not to live for ourselves but to live for Him. Praying on behalf of His name's sake:

- Seeks God's will
- Honors His name
- Set limits for the enemy

Praying on behalf of His name's sake affirms that God is sovereign.

It is a strong tactic of the enemy to get us to focus on ourselves and our problems. Should the enemy succeed, our prayers lack the consideration of God and of other people. We pray for answers that are self-centered and we demand to have our own way. However, when we recall that God is sovereign we reverse selfish prayers to prayers yielded to God. We pray, "God, use my life to make a name for You. 'For thou art my rock and my fortress; therefore for thy name's sake lead me, and guide me'" (Psalm 31:3).

God is Sovereign! This is what Paul tried to communicate to the sailors who were traveling with him on a boat en route to Rome. In Acts 27, Paul was on a ship with other prisoners traveling to Rome to answer charges against him. Paul had mentioned before they set sail that the voyage would result in damage and great loss. But the centurion was persuaded to continue forward. After setting sail, they were confronted by the violent wind called Euroclydon. The ship was caught in the storm. Fearing that the ship would crash into the rocks, they dropped the anchors and prayed for daylight. In an attempt to escape the ship, the sailors let down the lifeboat. "Paul said to the centurion and to the soldiers, Except these abide in the ship, ye cannot be saved; then the soldiers cut off the rope of the boat, and let her fall off" (v. 31-32).

The soldiers reached their limits. They concluded that the storm was greater than their strength and ability. Survival, in their minds, meant to escape. Have you ever been in a situation where you thought "escape" was the only viable answer? Was there ever a time when you just wanted "out?" The soldiers wanted out and the lifeboats were their way of escape. However, instead of escaping, the soldiers cut loose and released the lifeboats. The cutting and releasing of the lifeboats demonstrated reliance on God as their rescue.

Challenging times can make us feel as though we are caught in a storm. Life's pressures resemble heavy, violent winds. We are tossed to and fro. Sometimes our only recourse is to close our eyes and to pray for morning to come. We have weighed all of our options. We have considered all alternatives. In a desperate moment, we stop and realize that God is sovereign, and the heavy wind ceases to roar. So we cut our lifeboats—we stop relying on people and we rely on God. We confirm within our spirit that God is bigger than any challenge we could ever face. He is our rescue—He will deliver!!!

The Millionaire Christian profits from Spiritual Capital.
During challenging times,
Sovereignty
Verifying God as the Supreme and Ultimate Authority
Is
Spiritual Capital

Sovereignty Is Spiritual Capital

REVIEW QUESTIONS

1. God's name carries p_____ and a_____.

2. During challenging times, Jesus is our _____.

3. During challenging times we must recall God's _____.

4. Match the following:

   a. Jehovah Jireh   The Peace Maker

   b. Jehovah Rapha   The Advocator

   c. Jehovah Tsid-Kenu   The Provider

   d. Jehovah Shalom   The Most High God

   e. Jehovah Nissi   The Healer

   f. Jehovah El Elyon   The Protector

5. Convert your prayers. Write your prayer request on the blank below:

   God, _____ for your Name's sake

   God, _____ for your Name's sake

   God, _____ for your Name's sake

   God, _____ for your Name's sake

   God, _____ for your Name's sake

6. Recall a time when you cut your lifeboat and stopped relying on people and relied on God instead.

_____

_____

7. Complete the following resume testifying of God's victories in your life.

   Example:

Year	Challenging Time	God's Victory
1996	Received doctor's report that should have a hysterectomy	Had two full term pregnancies

God's Victories For:

Name: _____

Address: _____

City, State, Zip Code: _____

Telephone Number: _____

Sovereignty Is Spiritual Capital

Year	Challenging Time	God's Victory

*Use a separate sheet of paper if additional space is needed

Take a moment and journal to God your thoughts, revelations, or reflections received from reading this Key Attribute.

Reflection: _____

_____

_____

_____

_____

Summary

BY NOW YOU understand that the status of a Millionaire Christian has nothing to do with money. People seeking money believe that money gives them a sense of empowerment. Some even believe that money is the key that opens doors to their world of dreams. Others believe that with money they could have the best: the best house, the best car, the best school for their kids. What some people believe about money and what money can do for them, the Millionaire Christian believes that the birth, death, and resurrection of Jesus Christ can do more than what money could ever do. For the Millionaire Christian, money is not the answer.

During challenging times, the Millionaire Christian's spiritual response is total DEPENDENCE on God as the Source to supply all of their needs. The Millionaire Christian celebrates God and is obedient in all things (2 Corinthians 2:9). The Millionaire Christian has a surplus of energy because the same Spirit that raised Jesus from the dead dwells within. The Millionaire Christian retains a preoccupation with God and believes that God supplies what's needed and how much is needed. Moreover, if something is lacking, then it is not needed. The Millionaire Christian has validated the existence of God and needs no evidence or proof. The Millionaire Christian has a "more than a conqueror mentality"—with God, nothing is IMPOSSIBLE!

During challenging times, the Millionaire Christian refuses to believe a lie. They wait for God's best. God is in the driver's seat and is the only force that is capable of shaping, directing, and influencing. The Millionaire Christian petitions God based on His reputation and the name He established. The Millionaire Christian prays, "God, use my life to make a name for You. 'For thou art my rock and my fortress; therefore for thy name's sake lead me, and guide me'" (Psalm 31:3).

In conclusion, I want to end with this last thought. The Millionaire Christian recommits to Jesus Christ. Over time, stress, anxiety, frustration, and disappointment associated with challenging times builds up. Recommitment reaffirms and rekindles our love for Jesus Christ. According to Revelation 2:5, there are three R's to recommitment:

1. Remember
   - The times when Love intervened
   - The grace bestowed upon us when we did not deserve it
   - The mercy shown when we did not receive the consequence we rightly deserved

Summary

- The prayers that were answered and the dreams that were made realities
- The miracles and the blessings

2. Repent
   - Acknowledge and confess our separation from God
   - Humble ourselves—seek restoration
   - Stop the actions and behaviors serving as barriers that separate us from God
   - Destroy and cut off any and everything that contributed to our separation from God
   - Fear God—recognize God's position, presence, and power

3. Redo
   - Rekindle the hunger and thirst to become like Christ
   - Recapture the zeal of being chosen, royal, holy, and peculiar
   - Renew an attitude of praise and thanksgiving
   - Revisit the meaning and significance of the death of Jesus and His blood that was shed for us
   - Re-strategize our purpose and mission to win souls—be an effective witness for Christ

Now that you have read this book, I recommend that you recommit (Remember, Repent, and Redo) on a daily basis. Recommitment is not renewing our salvation. On the contrary, recommitment is reiterating to the enemy our decision to put our sins, mistakes, and regrets behind and to present our bodies as a living sacrifice, holy and acceptable unto God, which is our reasonable service (Romans 12:1).

Congratulations on discovering the Millionaire in you.
Your life will never be the same!

Summary

End of the Day Meditation & Review Journal

Meditation consists of critiquing and reviewing your daily actions and interactions to ensure alignment to scripture. Complete this review journal at the end of your day. This Meditation & Review Journal is designed to connect day-to-day living to the will of God.

Day: _____ Date: _____

Start Time: _____ End Time: _____

Today I prayed for: _____

_____

Scriptures I read today that supported my prayers were:

_____

_____

Scriptures God placed on my heart today were:

_____

_____

God can call me a "good and faithful servant" because today I _____

_____

_____

I bless God for this day because He:

_____

_____

I ask forgiveness for:

_____

_____

Tomorrow I will allow God to direct my paths to complete the following goals:

_____

_____

_____

Summary

90 Day Prayer Journal

"Pray without ceasing"
—I Thessalonians 5:17

Complete each blank. Do not begin your answers with the following words: "I," "Because," "God is," or "God, you have done."

Day# _____

Opening Salutation:

Who is God to you?

_____

_____

Acknowledgment of Praise:

What is God doing for you?

_____

_____

Acknowledgment of Power:

What is God able to do?

_____

_____

Acknowledgment of Authority:

Why should you obey God?

_____

_____

Acknowledgment of Dependence:

Why do you need God?

_____

_____

Acknowledgment of Righteousness:

What does God control in your life?

_____

_____

Acknowledgment of Forgiveness:

What sin do you need to confess?

_____

_____

Summary

Whose sin do you need to forgive?

_____

_____

Acknowledgment of Request:

What is it that you want God to do?

_____

_____

What scripture(s) supports your request?

_____

_____

Ending Salutation:

What is it that you understand about God?

_____

_____

Now put it all together. This time include words like "I," "Because," "God is," and "God you have done," etc.

God, you are _____ to me. I give you praise for _____. Through your power you _____

_____, *You hold Supreme Authority in my life because* _____.

I surrender total dependence on you because _____.
God, your righteousness controls my _____.
God, forgive me for _____ *as I also forgive* _____. *God, I bodily come before your throne and ask* _____ *as (put scripture(s) here)* _____.

I thank you, God, for you are _____.

In Christ Jesus' name I pray.

Amen.

_____   _____
Your signature   *Date*

Example:

Opening Salutation:

Who is God to you? Faithful, Caring, Deliverer

Acknowledgment of Praise:

What is God doing for you? Delivering, Blessing, Protecting

Acknowledgment of Power:

What is God able to do? Meet Needs, Desires, Keep me

Summary

Acknowledgment of Authority:

Why should you obey God? Know, Fear, Love Him

Acknowledgment of Dependence:

Why do you need God? Can't live without, Dead without

Acknowledgment of Righteousness:

What does God control in our life: Thoughts, Mind, Heart

Acknowledgment of Forgiveness:

What sin do you need to confess? Disobeyed when told to give $20 and only gave $10

Whose sin do you need to forgive: Sister for lying on me

Acknowledgment of Request:

What is it that you want God to do? Healing from headaches

What scripture(s) supports your request? Isaiah 53:5

Ending Salutation:

What is it that you understand about God? Awesome, Healer, Savior

Now put it all together. This time include words like "I," "Because," "God is" and "God, you have done," etc.

God, you are faithful and caring. You are a deliverer to me. I give you praise for delivering me, blessing me, and protecting me. Through your power you meet my needs and desires, and you keep me. You hold Supreme Authority in my life because I know you, fear you, and love you. I surrender total dependence on you because I can't live without you and I am dead without you. God, your righteousness controls my thoughts, heart, and mind. God, forgive me for disobeying when you told me to give $20 dollars in church and I only gave $10, as I also forgive my sister for accusing me of wearing her dress when I did not. God, I bodily come before your throne and ask for healing from these terrible headaches, as Isaiah 53:5 says, "But he was wounded for our transgressions, he was bruised for our iniquities, the chastisement of our peace was upon him, and with his stripes we are healed."

I thank you, God, for you are Awesome and my Healer and my Savior.

In Christ Jesus' name I pray.

Amen.

_____   _____

Your signature   *Date*

Summary

Recommitment Journal
Remember—Repent—Redo

Reference the recommitment examples in the summary to help you complete your Recommitment Journal.

On this day, _____

I Remember:

_____

_____

_____

I Repent:

_____

_____

_____

I Redo:

_____

_____

_____

Affirmations

As a man thinks in his heart, so is he.
—Proverbs 23:7

Life experiences can program us to think contrary to God's word. However, I Corinthians 2:16 says that we have the "mind of Christ," therefore we reason, think, feel, and judge just like Christ. An affirmation is a declaration of the truth. Below are scriptural affirmation statements, our weapons of warfare designed to cast down imaginations and every high thing that exalts itself against the knowledge of God, and bring into captivity every thought to the obedience of Christ (2 Corinthians 10:5). For the next six weeks, repeat each affirmation statement three times a day. At the end of each week, reflect on your outcomes, experiences, and revelations.

Week (1)

1. I am confident that God will answer my prayers because before I call on God He answers and while I am yet speaking God hears me (Isaiah 65:24).
2. I have control over every situation in my life and I overcome every opposition that would dare to come against me through the love of God which is in Christ Jesus (Romans 8:37).
3. Because I behave in a manner that is correct before God, I make progress and I complete every endeavor I pursue (Psalm 37:23).

Summary

Week (2)

1. I overcome the opposition. I confront my challenges. I have no fear and I endure to the end because God is with me (Joshua 1:9).
2. I am confident that God will complete, perfect, and develop me (Philippians 1:6).
3. I am consciously aware of God at all times (Colossians 3:2).

Week (3)

1. I abide in Christ. Therefore I am complete in my spirit, soul, and mind (Colossians 2:9-10).
2. I trust God with all of my heart and I have no confidence in my flesh (Psalm 118:8).
3. When I have considered all of my options, and I don't know how my change will come, God is God and God is able (Luke 18:27).

Week (4)

1. I have the spirit of power, love, and a sound mind (I Timothy 1:7).
2. People will not silence me. I am aware of God's presence in my life and I will testify about what He has done for me (Psalm 118:17).
3. I defeat evil with good (Romans 12:21).

Week (5)

1. I love the Lord and obey His voice (I John 5:3).
2. I will bless the Lord at all times; His praise shall continually be in my mouth (Psalm 34:1).

3. Sin does not control me. I have favor with God (Romans 6:14).

Week (6)

1. Nothing can separate me from the love of God which is in Christ Jesus (Romans 8:9).
2. I am not condemned. I hear the Spirit speak to me and I obey (Romans 8:1).
3. I am holy and I glorify God in my body (I Corinthians 6:19-20).

www.ingramcontent.com/pod-product-compliance
Lightning Source LLC
Chambersburg PA
CBHW030325080526
44584CB00012B/721